The Road Ahead – My Way

Barry B. Read

ISBN: 978-0-244-02027-9

Published by

Lodge Books
25 South Back Lane
Bridlington
www.lodgebooks.co.uk

Prologue

"Well, don't get serious about me sweetheart, I'm going to be a long-distance lorry driver, so you won't see much of me."

"Oh, and what makes you think I want to see much of you?"

"Well sweetheart, most of my other one night stands think that."

"I've got news for you mister, I'm not a one night stand and never will be. Certainly not for you anyway."

Wow, I thought, this is new. How do I overcome this? I know she is attracted to me, and she certainly appeals to me. Come on Barry, a new approach is needed.

After coming through the swinging saloon-type doors of the Spa Royal Hall in Bridlington, at the usual Saturday night hop, and fuelled by a couple of 'Bass Red Caps', I made my way towards the dance floor looking for a likely candidate to satisfy my urge. Usually I was quite successful at this particular venue. Swaggering, or maybe staggering, I noticed this rather tasteful young girl stood against one of the pillars, looking quite stunning and seeming to be available, dressed in a tight green sweater, with boobs pointing out, and a flowing black skirt. Hey, I thought, now lucky lady, come on let's get it on tonight.

Full of confidence, I pulled her on to the dance floor to show her all my best moves, but something must have gone wrong as she didn't seem to be suitably impressed. What's wrong Barry? The usual approach clearly isn't working tonight. However, with reluctance on her part, I managed to get her outside, but a kiss and a cuddle were not forthcoming. Um, I thought, what next? No way was I going to succeed with my usual Saturday night desires.

"OK love," I said. "What about Tuesday night at the Regal Picture House? Seven p.m., see you inside, back row. (That meant I didn't pay for them.)

What I didn't know at that time was that this was her first date and, somehow, she wasn't totally impressed at either seeing me

1

inside or paying for herself. Her expectations came higher. Reluctantly, I agreed to meet her outside and, as far as I can remember, we each paid for ourselves – not too bad I suppose. I was smitten with her and have loved my 'Sandra' ever since.

Woolworths staff dance 1957. Barry and Sandra in our courting days.

Chapter One

I was born on 20th December 1938 to my parents, Jack Burnham Read and Virginia May Read (my mother's maiden name was Wise), although I found out fifty years later that I was conceived out of wedlock. But at least they were married when I came along at The Avenue maternity hospital in the Old Town of Bridlington. As far as I am aware we lived for a short period of time, along with my grandmother (Gladys Child), at the respective gatehouses to Sewerby Hall grounds, before moving to number 18 Havelock Crescent, with my gran moving to number 36. This was where I called home until I was eighteen years old.

Times then were very hard. The Second World War had just begun, food was rationed, treats were non-existent, black-outs were in force and everyday existence was a bonus. Although Bridlington was not a main target for the invading German Luftwaffe, because of its coastal position on the North Sea the Luftwaffe flew over the town on its way to bomb the ports of Hull and Liverpool and the industrial areas of Leeds and other northern towns. Any unused bombs were exploded over Bridlington on their return.

Many of the British Air Force were stationed near Bridlington at places such as Carnaby, Catfoss and Lissett, where Sandra's father (James Miller) was stationed and consequently met Sandra's mother (Marjorie Pashby). They later, after the war years, were divorced and Sandra was raised by her grandparents, Richard and Mary Pashby.

My dad, although not a frontline soldier, was a dispatch motorcycle rider to the Home Guard, due I believe to his eyesight – maybe not the best quality for a motorcyclist anyway!

Like all the houses in Havelock Crescent, number 18 had no inside toilet, and toilet paper was cut in strips from old newspapers and hung behind the privy door. There was no bathroom, just a tin bath hung behind the scullery door which was used once a week (usually a Friday night) with water boiled on the open fire and for all of us to use – my mum, dad, my sister Diane and normally me last. Any other washing of ourselves was done via the scullery sink in cold water.

One memory that will never leave me is of the winter of 1947 when everything was frozen and even the back door to reach the outside loo couldn't be opened because of the snow. At least I couldn't go to school, which was at Oxford Street, although I quite enjoyed it and, even though I say it myself, I was quite bright. In the final term at the junior school, in Miss Jackson's class, I came top of the class, which should have made me eligible to sit my Eleven Plus. Unfortunately, or otherwise, Mr O'Brian who was the headmaster excluded me from taking it, and when my mum complained she was told that I was not 'grammar school material' as I was rough, even though another in the same classroom as myself was allowed to sit it and passed. Imagine that sort of discrimination now.

So I went on to St Georges School and really enjoyed myself there. I made some lifelong friends, played football for my house and school teams, represented school at high jump, where I had a unique style by jumping from a forward position rather than using a sideways technique. Once my teacher, Mr Johnnie Walker, said, "Read, you could jump a farmyard gate." Hmm, if only now.

While in my early years, from nine to twelve, to earn my pocket money I made a two-wheel carrier barrow and, along with others, I would go to the likes of the railway station or the bus station and offer to carry the suitcases of visitors coming on holiday, as Bridlington in those days was a very popular and enterprising guest house location, and I even took bookings for the following week when the families were returning home.

During the winter, my barrow was still in use as I brought cinders from the gas house (all bagged and weighed) and was paid by the residents of Havelock Crescent. Another form of revenue came from collecting lemonade bottles for which I would receive threepence a bottle.

Also when I was a bit older, although still at school, I was a grocer's errand lad. I had a bike with a carrier at the front with a cardboard box laden with groceries for delivery anywhere within the town. This was normal and my mates did the same for either the local grocer or butcher. A far cry from the internet services of today. But maybe not, the end product is the same – home delivery, although not to present day standards.

I was regarded as quite a competent goalkeeper and played, when only fifteen to seventeen years of age, for the likes of Bridlington Amateurs, Trinity United and in the Sunday league for Dales, Gallaghers, Brid Fishermen, and was invited for trials with Wolverhampton Wanderers, the team of the time. But no way could I afford the expense involved. Who knows where that would have gone?

After leaving school at fifteen years of age, my first job was at Elsons Engineering on North Back Lane in Bridlington. But it wasn't for me – too dirty. I moved on to Cleggs, making fireplaces – another one that wasn't for me. Then out of the blue something else came up. My dad was lorry driving for Mr Arthur Petch who had four lorries, all on 'A' licences, that he had bought from BRS, which had been denationalised in 1951, after the Labour government of the day in 1947 had nationalised all free enterprise road transport along with other industries. The 'A' licence meant you could carry anything anywhere in the UK, whereas the 'B' licence vehicles had a 65-mile radius, and 'C' licence vehicles were restricted to carrying their own manufactured goods. My dad drove a petrol Commer QX 10-ton carrying capacity lorry and the main loads were from Cross Bone Fertilisers on Pinfold Lane in Bridlington to various farms. By then dad was, with respect, tiring and it was my job to load and unload the 8-stone bags of fertiliser. I also went with the other drivers and did the same for them. I loved it and found great delight in showing how strong I was.

SHB Transport (Service Haulage Bridlington) was the making of me and all I ever thought about was driving a lorry and dreamt of one day having one of my own. A dream that was later to come true, but at that time it seemed like a dream too far. SHB Transport then opened an office in Lambert Street, Hull where we loaded by hand vast amounts of timber mainly to deliver in the Birmingham

5

area. Then we reloaded with tractors and parts to bring back to Hull Docks for shipment to all parts of the world. Such was the need for British-built goods.

Moretons of Coventry were the main carriers of the time and could be seen all over with their pale green Commer TS3 artics with tractors on board. Another main clearing house agent we used was Hickenbottoms in Walsall who would load us back into the north-east with mainly steel.

Often we would go to London, a three-day round trip, loading back through Tower Hill Clearing House, and it was the norm to park up in the area and go on foot to their offices for an advice authorisation ticket. If that failed to find a load, we had a pocketful of pennies to telephone other agents to find out what they had and at what rate. In those days all the wharfs in the tower vicinity were buzzing with dock-related work. Hays Wharf and others thronged along the banks of the Thames, reaching as far as the old London Bridge. Lorries were queued up waiting for their turn to load to all parts of the UK.

Traffic was very congested as there were no weight restrictions for lorries and they could come and go as they pleased. The Thames embankment, especially on the north side, was a main transit route to the north and the west. Billingsgate fish market, Smithfield meat market, Fleet Street for newspaper publishing, Spitalfields fruit market, Borough market – I could go on. Oh what a magical thriving place for a young lad to be. Where else would I want to be? Let's see.

Without doubt my love of transport was also clouded by my image of myself as a groover. Every Saturday night at the Spa Royal Hall the big bands of yesteryear would appear i.e. Joe Loss, Eric Delany, Johnny Dankworth, Ted Heath. Wow, how we all enjoyed the glamour they exuded. The singers in those days were mega-stars and my overall favourite was Dickie Valentine and when he sang ladies swooned. Yes Barry, that's for me. So I had an audition with our local band leader, Eddie Harper, and was asked what I was going to sing. My rendition of 'Finger of Suspicion', my best interpretation, was hastily interrupted by Eddie with, "Boy, are you any good at football?" So my dreams of the big time were shattered.

Barry, my lovely mum and my sister Diana about 1944.

BRIGHAM   BRIDLINGTON

My dad served as a dispatch rider during the Second World War.

Chapter Two

For reasons not known to me, SHB Transport ceased trading and Mr Arthur Petch, whom I really admired, went to work as transport manager for a bakery company. By now I was eighteen years old and couldn't wait to learn to drive properly. So when a job as a warehouse delivery man, with the distinct possibility of learning to drive, came up, I took it.

Peters Wine & Spirit Merchants had their depot on Edgecliffe Villas near the railway bridge on Flamborough Road. I enjoyed being there as one of the benefits was, as they also supplied soft drinks, that I could drink as many bottles of Vimto and Sunfresh as I wanted – even today, still a favourite. My introduction to driving came with driving a 1-ton petrol, forward control, flatbed Austin with a huge rear door and very much 'suicide' cab doors.

For reasons I am unaware of, and it was the start of the blocking of the Suez Canal by President Nasser which obviously left in a critical state supplies of crude oil to the UK, learner drivers could drive unaccompanied. This suited me and my bosses, Mr George Gray and Mr R Earnshaw, as I could go out on deliveries around Bridlington and as far as Ravenscar, north of Scarborough, on my own.

Finally it came to my driving test, starting on Victoria Road in Bridlington. After some brief, pretty simple, road sign questions, I was told to proceed when I was ready. In those days especially, trucks didn't have indicator flashers, or the right/left leg that came from the side of the vehicle. The means of turning right was to put your arm out of the window, or to turn left, again to stick your arm out of the window in a rotating style. I took one look in the outside mirror, nothing coming, and off I went. Eek, I hadn't signalled my intention to go. Aagh, or words to that effect, I had failed from the start.

After thirty minutes or so, having returned to the office on Victoria Road, I looked glumly at the test inspector to receive my result. He pulled me up and told me in no uncertain terms about not signalling when moving off, but at least I seemed competent enough to be let loose. Back at Peters' yard I informed them of my good fortune.

"Good," said Mr Earnshaw. "Now get these orders loaded and delivered, you're behind already today."

In my haste to get back to the yard I had forgotten to take the 'L' plates off my beloved little truck, but once discovered I ripped them off and binned them, and within a couple of weeks I was promoted (although it was horrible to drive) to their other truck, a petrol 3-ton flatbed Ford.

Peters' main depot was in Francis Street, Hull and I occasionally went there to load when Bridlington stocks were low. How good I felt going to the big city on my own to fetch vital supplies. Peters' claim is that they first introduced Carlsberg to the UK, it being shipped from Denmark into Hull docks and then transported by one of the biggest transport companies in Hull, Quay Warehousing. Their maroon and cream tractor units, with twin-axled trailers, fully laden with the dusky red wooden boxes of Carlsberg lager were a sight to be seen and I looked at them in awe.

They also delivered directly to our Bridlington depot, where they had to reverse all the way down from Flamborough Road into our warehouse. I admired the skill of the regular drivers as they weaved their way through the open door of the warehouse, trying to get as near to the stack of stored red boxes to make it as easy as possible to handball into store. After unloading, with either a Sunfresh or Vimto for refreshment, I would wheedle as much information as possible from the drivers about their times on the road.

Other lorries made deliveries such as Bass and Schweppes, but without doubt my favourites were the light blue ERF 4-wheel lorries from Babycham. They looked splendid with their logo of a fawn. The orange, open-topped boxes housing the blue-topped bottles made for a magical scene. Babycham then was a popular ladies drink and the Babycham lorries travelled the whole of the

UK from their base in Shepton Mallett, deep in the heart of Somerset.

By this time, National Service was a must for all men aged eighteen, with those learning a trade deferred until they were twenty-one. I registered, but at that time I had sent for papers to emigrate to Australia on the £10.00 assisted passage as back then Oz wanted any able body, trade, profession or whatever – a far cry from today's would-bes. The thought of those wide open roads without the regulations we had in the UK beckoned me. However, my dad was reluctant to sign the approval papers, which was needed, although I'm pretty sure my mum had a big say in that. I can only presume that at this time compulsory call-up for National Service was being phased out and as I had emigration papers (although never submitted) I was overlooked. Good or bad, I will never know. My best mate Jack Sygrove, although younger than me, was called up.

Although I hadn't been looking for a regular girlfriend (previously I had quite enjoyed the platonic relationships with a considerable number of girls coming on holiday to Bridlington – as the saying was: ship 'em in, ship 'em out), I was getting rather keen on Sandra. So, it was maybe a good thing I didn't go to Oz. But who knows what could have been.

By now my sights were set on more distant places and bigger lorries to drive, and this time was looming, when the chance to drive a Bedford 5-ton lorry belonging to Bill Day came up. Well, the choice was already made. The job entailed going twice a week to Leeds to load coal briquettes and then making my way back to Bridlington selling them house to house. Loading the briquettes was a long, laborious task as they came up to you on a conveyor belt steaming hot. Basically they were made from coal dust slag and pressed together in a vat. Then I loaded them six at a time in rows ten high along the length of my lorry.

I would leave Bridlington at 5.00 a.m. on Mondays and Thursdays and Sandra somehow found the time to come with me; I dropped her off on The Headrow in Leeds while I went to load on Woodhouse Lane and picked her up later. On the way back to

Bridlington we drove via Market Weighton, Middleton on the Wolds, Driffield and various villages en route. Sandra, sporting a satchel-type money pouch, took the money from the various customers and was in charge of the cash while I did the labouring, stacking the briquettes where required. Bill Day trusted us implicitly, but by now his health was failing and the strain was telling.

I was, in turn, looking for other more demanding adventures to pursue. My dad was working for G E Mitchells in Bridlington, a bone and tallow business, and was driving what was my dream lorry – a Commer TS3 two-stroke flatbed 10-ton lorry with a matching 4-ton drawbar trailer. Wow! A job came up at Mitchells, which I applied for and was successful in getting. I was driving a diesel Thames lorry, collecting bones and residue from dead animals and taking it to the likes of Wiles Fertilisers at Beverley on a Wednesday, and every Monday going to Greenwoods in Halifax. Although a pretty disgusting load to carry I did enjoy it. The worst bit of all was collecting dead and rotten carcases infected by maggots from Bennie Websters at Beeford.

As I was young, nineteen years old, my thirst for showing how strong I was soon paid dividends as George, Mr Mitchell, bought a brand new Thames Trader (VBT 334) for me with very high sides which increased the loading capacity to eight or nine tons. I loved this truck, but my eyes were on dad's Commer and trailer. Somehow, I don't know how, my dad surrendered to my dreams and I took over the Commer and trailer. The work involved loading 45-gallon barrels of tallow (a residue from the fat extracted by boiling the bones) and taking the drums to the likes of Knights in Nottingham, Lever Brothers in Port Sunlight and Silverton in London. The dried bones also took me as far as Loanhead near Dalkeith, south of Edinburgh, and Crosfields in Warrington.

A whole new world opened up to me in those days. Any vehicle towing a trailer was restricted to a staggering 20 m.p.h. so journey times were long. Bearing in my I was only nineteen years old and not legally entitled to drive anything over three and a half tons unloaded I felt privileged. Mr George Mitchell was good to me and for that I thank him, as with his and Bill Day's confidence in me they certainly helped me to go forward.

Taken at the rear of what was Quartons Greengrocers which her stepfather Mr E Shipman owned; now the premises of Holiday Travel on Promenade. Early 1957.

Me with my Thames Trader VBT334. I was 18 years old and my first ever new lorry. Mr Mitchell had faith in me.

My dad, Kenny and me loading barrels of tallow at George Mitchells about 1947.

Me driving the Commer TS3 with trailer en route back from Dalkeith, Scotland.

Chapter Three

While I was employed at SHB Transport I couldn't help being enthralled by the likes of Nicholls Bros Transport, where the four brothers each had their own lorry and worked mainly for Crossbone Fertilisers. They would pip and wave as they made their way to Crossbones as I walked to the same place, never once stopping to give me a lift. One day, Barry!

Eventually I got a job with Nicholls Bros – Dick, Chris, Charlie and Brian. My lorry was a Morris commercial diesel which had the peculiar motion of the engine going backwards, so it had to be stalled before, I believe, it would have blown up. As power steering at that time was unknown, bouncing the front wheels off a kerb edge helped to turn the vehicle into lock. I was then upgraded to a Seddon four-wheel flatbed, mainly working for Medfords Corn Merchants, loading and transporting barley to the grain silos of the likes of Dobsons and Knapton Silos. These were all 16-stone bags of barley and, if you were lucky, an elevator would send up the sacks from where you would let them slide across the back of your shoulders and load them into place. Other than that a tractor would drop the sack on to the lorry floor and it was your job to knee the sack into place – no elevator or tractor meant using a winding-up barrow then jumping on to the lorry floor and placing into loaded position.

One day, when three of us were loading at Catnab Farm at the top of the notorious Garrowby Hill, I was the last to load for Dobsons. The others left way before me and went on their way via Driffield, a long way round. Right, I thought, I will beat them by going down Garrowby. The brakes then on trucks left a lot to be desired; they were only vacuum brakes, two pumps and that was your lot. Predictably, my lorry got away from me and by the time I reached the bottom I really was out of control and count myself as extremely fortunate to get away with it. I did get to Dobsons first, but received my first real bollocking from Dick for going down

Garrowby Hill with a loaded lorry. Eventually I upgraded to a petrol Commer 10-ton aluminium body lorry which had a full bench seat, although nights out were a rarity.

By now Sandra and I had married at Trinity Church in Bridlington on 3rd October 1959. The reception was at her grandparents' house on Windsor Crescent. It was a beautiful sunny day and our reception was nice but not elaborate. We went on honeymoon, staying in London near Victoria Station, from where on the Sunday morning we caught the train to Newhaven and then the ferry for Dieppe in France.

Neither one of us had ever ventured outside the UK so this was the beginning of an new adventure. The ferries of that time were not like the ro-ro ships of today and I can recall cars being hoisted by crane on to the deck. On arrival in Dieppe some four hours later, we caught the train to Paris and then travelled by taxi through Paris to another station from where we took the overnight sleeper to the French/Spanish border at Le Perthus. As Spain was still controlled by the Spanish dictator Franco, cross border trains did not exist so we had to walk in the no-man's land to undergo customs control. From there we caught a train to Barcelona central station, from where we took what I can only describe as a cowboy-style train with wooden slatted seats to Sitges. A taxi took us to our hotel, the Constantino, and we spent four days there before travelling back to Dieppe.

The return crossing was horrendous. A force-10 gale was in place and many people were very seasick. Fortunately for us a steward, when boarding the ferry, showed us to a down below cabin, also occupied by some Australian people on holiday, and we were okay. On our return to London, we stayed at the Mapleton Hotel in Trafalgar Square and saw the movie South Pacific at the Domino Cinema on Tottenham Court Road.

The following day we took a train back to Bridlington to start our married life at Sandra's grandparents' house on Windsor Crescent with about £6.00 to our name. My first experience abroad and my thirst for the continent had begun, although it would be several years before I ventured abroad again.

I stayed with Nicholls Brothers for about twelve months or so, but I was feeling unsettled so I left without another job to go to. I hitchhiked and found myself in Selby, a town which in those days hosted a considerable number of hauliers. Somehow I found my way to Holmes Lane where I came upon Onward Road Transport. Several lorries – AEC, ERF, Albion – were in the yard; I was impressed. They were all painted in Lincoln green with a big yellow badge on the front with the emblem TA (Transport Association) which was a nationwide organisation of reputable hauliers.

Full of confidence – this was where I wanted to be – I made my way to the upstairs office, where I was again immediately impressed by the maps on the walls pinpointing all the major towns and cities in the UK and a large scale graph indicating where all their lorries were. I introduced myself to Mr Clarkson, the Transport Manager, and after an interview he said he would employ me, but only if I found lodgings in the Selby area – Bridlington was too far away. Full of anticipation, I found temporary accommodation at the Station Hotel in Selby. I hitchhiked back to Bridlington and told Sandra my good news. I can't remember if she was pleased or not.

My first week at Onward began with me driving a Bedford (no driving test as to my capabilities), although my eyes were focussed on the big trucks. Nevertheless, I went to load at Sturges Chemicals just off Abbotts Road in Selby. Laden with kegs of citric acid, which was used as an ingredient in soft drinks, I left for the Nottingham and Birmingham areas, with six or so drops to complete. The main road out of Selby, the A19, took me into Doncaster, along the main street. There was much congestion as this was the A1 route going north and south. Then on I drove to Bawtry where the A641 took me over the Dukeries into Nottingham and from there on to Birmingham on the A38, to complete my deliveries on the following day. That night I stayed at the Dove Transport Cafe, feeling at last like a real lorry driver, among their company.

Eventually I graduated to an Albion Chieftain 4-wheel rigid, which I enjoyed driving much more as this was similar to the one Nicholls Bros had and which I had driven on several occasions, when collecting on a Saturday night, from York railway station, the Sunday newspapers that had come up from the London presses and then going on to deliver them to newsagents, starting in Pocklington, through various villages to Bridlington and finishing at about 5.00 a.m. in Filey.

Onward Transport was part of the W. Storry group which included Ackworth Transport, Wharf Transport in Stockport, Parkers Transport, Barnsley and a depot in Cambridge Heath Road, Bethnal Green, London. Ackworth was probably the biggest depot of all and the array of lorries with drawbar trailers was to me amazing. Their main work was from Lumbs of Castleford, which made glass bottles for the drinks trade. These included the likes of Watney Mann in London, Johnnie Walker Whisky in Kilmarnock, Scotland, Bass in Burton and many more. The bottle trade then was very industrious and we would also load from Jacksons in Knottingley to all points, loading two pallets high. Everything then had to be sheeted and roped to secure the load and, particularly because Jacksons' load was cardboard cartons, corner boards had to be fitted which meant, after sheeting, climbing on top again to the place the corner boards where you would anticipate the ropes going over, so as not to crush the cartons. It was very physical work, not like today's curtain-siders with shrink-wrapped pallets.

Just so I could drive the bigger trucks, for a short period of time I went on the 'trunk', which meant just driving to London (for eleven hours) or to Glasgow (for fourteen hours) through the night trying to sleep in digs during the day while a shunter tipped and reloaded your lorry. Although I suppose it was a good job for an older man, it was not for the likes of me, who enjoyed being more active.

Eventually, back on days, I volunteered to drive Onwards' Chinese Six (double steer) single-drive with a four-axle trailer. The steering was horrendous, so heavy that it took all my strength to manoeuvre it when shunting into place. Again I wasn't totally

20

suited as most of the work for this vehicle was to Liverpool docks, where at times you could queue up for two days waiting to unload. Then, Liverpool was a thriving seaport with ships loading and unloading wares from across the globe. So I felt restricted and opted for a newly furbished six-wheeled Albion. I enjoyed this. After some time I was offered and took on a new contract they obtained with a brand new Leyland Octopus eight-wheeler tanker, working from Saltend, Hull, delivering black oil to the industrial sites of Sheffield and High Marnham power stations. To be in the company of transport companies like Harold Woods was challenging, but again after approximately six months I needed to move on.

While on tanker work I became friendly with a driver from Arrow Bulk tankers in Lime Street, Hull. Their work was a lot more varied and he put in a good word for me and there my days at Onward Road Transport ended.

While at Onward my means of getting to and from Selby was to hitchhike and I was usually successful. But on one Saturday, in late afternoon, I set off from Selby to come back home, dressed in my green overalls with a logbook in hand and tried to hitch a ride. Nothing stopped, so I walked all the way from Selby to Bubwith Bridge, approximately eight miles or so. By this time it was getting dark and I was very apprehensive that I wouldn't get a ride. I was seriously thinking of going back to Selby and staying in my lorry for the weekend. Nearing the bridge a car approached. I held up my logbook hoping that the driver would stop. But, no. However, the lights on the bridge turned red and the driver waved a come-on sign to me. I started to run towards him but was aware from past experience that once you did this they would take off and leave you stranded and chuckle to themselves. However, he waited for me and asked where I was going. When I said Bridlington, to my surprise and great delight he said, "So am I," and he dropped me off at home.

At that time I smoked, but from that day onwards I stopped, saved the money and bought my first car, an Austin 8 – FAK 937.

In relation to my time at Onward I must thank my very good friends: Arthur Gill who still lives in Whitley Bridge; and George Goodall from Barlby with whom on lots of occasions I stayed overnight.

Chapter Four

After my interview with a Mr Tomlinson who was the M.D. and, I believe, an ex-brigadier, I was offered a job as a relief driver on varied contracts they held. The only stipulation was that I must live in the Hull area, which I agreed to. Back home I went to tell Sandra my good news and that we were moving to Hull. Totally excited (I don't think so) she agreed and we found ourselves renting a downstairs flat at 441 Spring Bank West in Hull.

Arrow Bulk, as I said, had various contracts and I was introduced to them. Each vehicle was designated to a particular product such as rubber latex, a white sticky substance which was predominantly delivered to the London Rubber Company to make 'French letters'. Others included paraffin wax, going down empty to Llandacy in South Wales to load, which made Tic Tak firelighters in Hull, sulphate lye a black sticky fluid for making bricks and other vehicles on edible oil contracts. My favourite lorry was a Foden eight-wheeler (which I still have a model of) on the Llandacy run.

Unfortunately I fell out with one of the drivers and, having him pinned against a wall threatening to punch his lights out, I was reprimanded. So I decided, before I was sacked, to leave. Sandra was not duly impressed and was by now heavily pregnant with our son Kevin. This gave her the opportunity to come back to Bridlington, as she was never happy living in Hull, where we moved into our first owned property, a three-bed semi at 21 East Road.

Now I was saddled with a £2,750 mortgage for the next twenty-five years – what seemed a fortune then. In the meantime I had secured a job with Valley Transport, a leading Hull-based company owned by Stewart, Esplen & Greenhough on a contract with Ideal Standard delivering heating radiators to distributors and sites throughout the UK. I liked it here as the work involved heavy lifting and some way-out delivery points. I was there for about six months or so, but inevitably (it must be me) I got itchy feet and felt like a change. A friend of mine, Bobby Brown, told me of a job going at Fred Wrights in Selby to drive an eight-wheeler Atkinson with a Gardner 6LW engine (FFA 937). With Sandra and Kevin safely tucked up in our new house, off I went in my little Austin 35 van to meet the transport manager, Mr Albert Whiteley. We got on great together and after a short interview I was given the job.

So began my longest employment ever. I loved it at Fred Wrights; Mr Wright was a lovely man and his brother Charlie became a lifelong friend. Alf the fitter took to me and I could practically have anything I wanted for my eight-wheeler Atki. The other drivers, all characters in their own right, were good to work with and again I made good friends.

Fred's fleet varied, but all were second-hand lorries, ranging from four-wheelers, six-wheelers and eight-leggers. Most of his work was second-hand, mainly through LEP Transport, based in Goole, and Flowers Transport in York. Loads were to all parts of the country and, in the main, each driver found his own loads back home by contacting their own preferred clearing house. This suited me perfectly. Unlike Onward Transport, where I had to have digs in Selby, at Fred's it didn't matter, so I would load from say London, Cumpsty the forwarding agent on Albany Road, just off the Old Kent Road, I would load to the likes of Scotland or South Wales and back. Where my Atki would only do 30 m.p.h., by the time I had done a round trip my week was up.

Sleeping arrangements were such that most drivers, including me, took a suitcase loaded with a change of going-out clothes with them, and the case substituted as part of your bed by propping it up against the passenger window. As the engine was literally just a big hump in the cab you were able to sprawl over it and rest your head on the case. Surprisingly I always slept quite well, but bearing in mind a working week contained as many as ninety to a hundred hours. These were actually worked, not calculated running times and I still have the wage slips to prove it. A long way away from today's regulations; then, you ate when hungry and slept when tired. Yes, without doubt, Fred's suited just fine.

24

As you found a lot of your return loads when contacting a clearing house, the first thing you did was to confirm a destination and the rate. Thinking back, how the hell did Fred make any money, as a guide rate from London to Glasgow was in the region of £1 15/- a ton on a cap load of sixteen tons, relevant to your tonnage capacity.

As we didn't have a phone at home, at least once a week I would ring Sandra's mum. I recall I rang to be told that Kevin, probably two or three years old, had badly burnt his hand on an electric fire while Sandra was in a shop. I was in London loaded for Dunbarton, but made the decision to come home in my Atki, completely off-route. I arrived home in the early hours of the morning, spent the rest of the day with them and set off at about 6 p.m. to go to Dunbarton.

I had only gone ten miles towards Driffield (Nafferton Slack) when a tyre burst on the inside rear axle. Cursing my luck and my stupidity, I proceeded to set about the task of changing wheels. It was now dark so I lit a few diesel rags and laid then at the rear offside in an attempt to, in the first instance, see what I was doing, as the spare wheel carrier was at the back and under the body. Quite by chance this Thames Trader tipper truck stopped and out stepped the driver, Fred Haines, who I had never met before. Seeing my plight, he drove his truck on to the grass verge with his headlights shining on to the blown tyre and proceeded to undo the wheel studs while I laid under the back to take out my spare wheel.

Suddenly there was an almighty crash and a car drove straight into the back end of my lorry, causing the spare wheel carrier and the crashed car to trap me. Confusion erupted; although I wasn't particularly hurt, I couldn't move. Eventually the police arrived, followed by the fire engine and to my relief they somehow got me out. Seemingly the lady driver hadn't seen my lorry and drove straight into the back of me. She was hysterical, but after what seemed like ages the police calmed her down. When it was discovered she had her father in the back of her car and he was slumped (no seatbelts then) and moaning, with blood streaming from his head, an ambulance was called and he was taken to

Driffield Hospital. The police took all our details and I pointed at the oily rags I had lit, which by now were extinguished (no hazard indicator lights were fitted to my lorry).

Eventually, Fred Haines and I changed the wheels over. After thanking him for his efforts I then set off for Dunbarton. By this time it was at least 10 p.m. and I was really upset and certainly had a troubled mind. By the time I got to Londonderry on the A1 I had had enough. It was after midnight and I was going to get the sack for being so far off-route, but I thought what the hell. I stopped, lifted the engine cover and cut the plastic pipe running from the lift pump to the main pump and then proceeded only a short distance before the engine cut out and I coasted to a stop. Knackered is the word, and I fell fast asleep. Oh, I had viewed a spot where I could stop safely before cutting the pipe; I certainly didn't want another mishap.

At about 8 a.m. I found a phone and rang to say what had happened previously and that the Atki had broken down. Thankfully, Charlie answered. He said he would come out to me and tow me back to the depot. A hearty breakfast at Lawsons transport cafe at Londonderry seemed apt, knowing this was the end of my days at Fred's. Charlie took one look at the plastic pipe and said, "You have cut this, haven't you Barry?" No good lying to Charlie, he was a lot smarter than me and I had a great deal of respect for him. I told him how I felt and how stupid and scared I was. He already knew about the wheel and the crashed car as the police had been there first thing.

Charlie towed me back to the depot, where both Fred and Albert gave me a very discerning look. Thinking this was it, I started taking my things out of my lovely Atki. Both Fred and Charlie came to me and said, "What are you doing?"

Fred, a gentleman, as ever, politely said, "Barry, why didn't you just come back here, leave your lorry and go home? Don't do anything like this again." I later found out that Charlie had stood up for me. Wonderful people; the very best.

Unfortunately, that was far from the end of the tale. The lady driver's father, who was injured, died in hospital from his injuries, mainly because he was a Jehovah's Witness and wouldn't have blood transfusions.

Fred Wright, like many other hauliers, was having to change over to articulated lorries as the transport industry developed. So Fred bought six new Leyland and Dodge tractor units with fifth wheel coupled trailers. I got one of the Leylands which suited me fine, although it was far from comfortable to sleep in. One job I particularly liked, during the pea season, was delivering to the London fruit markets, Spitalfields and Borough Market, but my favourite was Covent Garden. This was right in the London theatre land and after the shows all the toffs (people got dressed up then) went to the various tea bars that thronged around the market. I enjoyed mingling with them and found the whole scene so interesting.

The market traders were unique in that when you arrived in the market, runners would come up to you with a ticket and take what was stated on the ticket. They seemed to come from all over, which was a bit confusing, but an honesty among them meant the final count was correct and your delivery notes clearly signed as correct. From there you would drive to Albany Road, have a few hours kip, wait for Cumpsty's to open and give you reload instructions, reload whatever, then you were off again to wherever.

Eventually Fred bought a new Seddon artic unit with a Gardner 150 engine and a tandem axle Boden trailer. I was fortunate to be assigned to it. I loved this truck and took a great deal of pride in it, although a couple of other drivers moaned about me getting it as they were more senior in terms of length of service there. I did have a bit of a reputation as a day and nighter, not afraid to make my point of view known to anyone, so most of the criticism was made behind my back.

Alas my hunger for working beyond the limits came to haunt me. I had reloaded in Glasgow, rang the office to tell them what I was loaded with and where for. It was a Friday, I was offered to come and change trailers in the yard and take a load of alkathene to British Visqueen in Stevenage and come back empty on the Saturday morning. By the time I got back to the yard and changed trailers it was past midnight when I set off again. I suppose I was thinking, why did I volunteer for this, I could be having and easy Saturday morning in the yard. However, off I went. Unfortunately, fatigue took over and by the time I reached Stibbington on the A1 I must have dozed off while driving. All of a sudden there was an almighty bang as I crashed the nearside of my truck into the offside of this massive low-loader trailer. From there I veered off into the central reservation on one of the very few bits of dual-carriageway on the A1 at that time. I completely lost control, the front offside of the trailer hit the rear of the cab and the whole outfit came to a sudden stop. All I can remember was waking up in Peterborough Hospital.

Apparently I had been thrown out of the cab and knocked unconscious, an ambulance had been called and there I was, bruised and battered, but in a lot healthier state than my Seddon and Boden. The cab, which was basically wood struts with metal surrounds, was completely crumpled and I can count myself extremely fortunate – one more of my nine lives. The trailer I had crashed into belonged to Annis of Hayes and was used as a tank carrier. As it was wider than a normal trailer it partly protruded from the lay-by it was parked in on to the road. Charlie Wright came down to bring me home. What would I have done without him during my time at Fred's.

I was off work for a few days, but was soon back. For months, even a year later, every time I went by the scene of the accident the alkathene pellets could be seen in and around the central reservation. Eventually the Seddon was rebuilt and handed back to me. In the meantime Fred had not really said much about my accident, but I did suspect there was something he wanted to say. Three or four months later I was delivering to a steel stockholders in Walsall. It was fairly busy and there was not much room there, when all of a sudden I felt a bang on the nearside front wing of my truck. Jumping down from my trailer, I saw a guy with a fork truck against the side of my truck. I was fuming, but to make matters worse, he just didn't seem to give a monkey's. Losing my temper, I pulled him from his fork truck and hit him. As he lay on the ground bleeding profusely from a distorted nose and screaming for help, I have to admit I lost it and grabbed him again. By then others had arrived on the scene and I was held back by them. The whole yard came to a standstill, some wanted to call the police, but the shop steward, seemed to think for whatever reason that it was not a good idea, however I and all Fred Wright's drivers would not be allowed there again.

I was only half unloaded and had to make a phone call back to the office to explain the circumstances, to be told to bring the part load back home. Driving back into the yard, both Fred and Charlie bounded over to me. It was the first and only time I ever saw Fred lose his rag. He really laid into me, which was probably part of the frustration he had stored up from my accident. A couple of hours later he came up to me, put his arm round me and was the gentleman, as ever. Between Alf, Charlie and myself we rectified the damage incurred on my truck.

A regular meeting place for Fred's drivers was on Back Church Lane, just off Commercial Road in London's East End, where we would park up. Sometimes, after the pea job to the markets and after reloading we could be finished by early afternoon, and I would quite often go for relaxation to the Turkish Baths on Mile End Road; I enjoyed that.

I would have a meal at Bray's transport cafe, then some entertainment at the Red Lion pub where there is a plaque on the wall saying 'Dick Turpin made his famous horseback ride to York from here'. This was where I saw my first go-go dancers, which was quite amusing as the girls came through a trap door and danced on the bar to rapturous cheers and applause from the locals, made up with drivers from all parts of the UK. The area around here is known as 'Gardners Corner' and even then a few of the buildings remained destroyed and blitzed from the Second World War bombings. Quite a few eccentrics lived among the remains and were noted for their antics; one of them especially pulled on a rope tied behind him several very large bundles of old newspapers, just like a road train. He was also very aggressive.

Yes, looking back, the happiest and most carefree working days of my life were spent at Fred Wright's. I made some great friends, in particular Dave Booker, Bill (Slim) Aldrid, Pete Carling and many others – all characters, a great team – and, first and foremost, Charlie Wright.

At Fred Wrights with my lovely Atki FFA 937 loading alongside 'Cockney Bob's' Atki with crates of oranges from Hull Docks for London markets. That's me with the sheet walking back to cover my load.

Chapter Five

Eventually I left Fred's after about eight years, with the intention of bettering myself. I got to know that a new freezer factory was being built in Cayton on the outskirts of Scarborough. So, late one Saturday, I called to the new site to enquire if they needed drivers. The security man on the gate told me that the transport, once the factory was operational, was being undertaken by Humber McVeigh Transport from Grimsby.

During the next week I rang the Grimsby office of Humber and was invited on the following Saturday for an interview with overall transport manager, Mr Dave Marsh, known locally, as I found out late, as 'Marshy'. I arrived at the Pyewipe Industrial Estate in Grimsby with Sandra, Kevin and Frances in my green Ford Capri for 10 a.m. I couldn't help being impressed with the array of fridge lorries parked at the entrance to the massive depot, both AEC Mercury and Mandator tractor units all coupled up to four-in-line fridge boxed trailers, all painted in a splendid green and red with gold-painted Humber logo.

After the relevant interview I was accepted and told I would be the first driver employed at the Scarborough depot for McCains. I took my time to look around the very impressive yard and garage facilities: a drive-through wash, not a hosepipe and a bucket and brush. Humber had also taken over McVeigh's Transport and they were parked up in their deep blue livery. Humber also had contracts with Birds Eye and they had lorries in their colours and logos. To say I was excited about the prospects is to put it mildly.

I found my way to Grimsby to pick up my brand spanking new AEC Mercury with a two-axle trailer with bright shiny aluminium sides sporting the McCains logo. First I caught the train to Hull, then on to the Hull-New Holland Humber ferry and, after some messing about, I arrived at Pyewipe. After some instructions on how to operate the fridge, I then went on to Grimsby docks to load frozen products for Scarborough. At that time all products came from Canada as the Scarborough site was far from full production.

Although I was the first driver to be employed for the McCain contract, Harry Tinker, who was already employed came to Scarborough, and three other drivers were taken on a bit later: Brian Carr, Dave Leach and Eddie Tully.

Eventually I was offered and took over a brand new Guy Big J, with a 150 Gardner engine with a double-axle sixteen-pallet trailer, again with shiny bright aluminium sides painted with the McCain logo all in glaring canary yellow; it certainly looked impressive. Maybe this was a mistake, as this and another were basically employed to transport products to and fro between Scarborough and Grimsby. I felt restricted and yearned for the uncertainties I was used to.

I got on well with the Grimsby drivers and one night, with another driver, stayed at Harry Tinker's flat and had a night out in Scarborough. After a late night we were late up and all of us had a 5 a.m. start. Harry, a single but divorced guy, had a lovely traditional white Jaguar car – running boards, the lot. As I say, late up, we dashed downstairs, all dressed in bright green overalls (Humber dress code) each carrying a suitcase into Harry's car and made off at speed. By the time we got near Cayton the police had a roadblock and we were brought to a halt. It took a bit of explaining, but seemingly someone had reported us as extremely suspicious and alerted the police. They must have thought we had pulled a job somewhere; even the police saw the humorous side of it.

However my time at Humber was quite short, as not only was I the first driver to be employed, I was also the first to be sacked. On one of the few occasions I was on another delivery, I went to Liverpool, rang up to say I was empty and couldn't get back to Scarborough as my driving time would be up at York, knowing full well that I was going to park up in Bridlington and book a night out on expenses. I parked my truck outside my mum and dad's on Havelock Crescent and went out for a drink at The Ship Inn with Sandra. Next morning about 6 a.m. I made my way to Scarborough. What I didn't know was that the manager Duggie and his foreman, Harry Askew, were sat behind The Dotterell pub and monitored me going past. When I put my logsheets in later that day, I was sacked for being off-route and claiming expenses. I appealed to Marshy but to no avail. Stupid, yes I know, although I have no excuse and I suppose it was my own fault. But on every previous occasion this guy Harry Askew, who came from Grimsby and made foreman, and Duggie turned a blind eye to such things as we were all doing the same. Harry Askew changed all that, but a couple of years later I was told he had been sacked for irregularities – poetic justice.

Although my first instinct was to go back to Fred Wright's, somehow I didn't want to feel I was using them. A job at Pete Fisher's was available, driving a two-stroke Foden artic, a really nice lorry with an amazing whining sound and with a twelve-speed epicycle gearbox. You really needed at least three hands to drive it comfortably as the manual gearstick was floor-mounted but the range change lever was to the right hand side of the steering wheel, with three positions – high, mid-range and low – while trying to steer at the same time; and no power assisted steering then.

The yard was at Gristhorpe, not far from Scarborough, and consisted of a large storage bay and farm buildings. My first day there, I asked one of the other drivers where I could wash my hands. His reply: "Back of cow-shed, there's a tap with caud water." What a comedown from the lovely warm toilets with hot running water at McCains. The job itself was reasonably okay; Fisher's did most of the dock delivery work for Dale Electric who made electrical generators which were shipped worldwide. This was good clean work and to my taste; what I didn't like was the farm-related work, when one day I had been to load sugar beet pulp – massive twelve-stone bags of residue from sugar beet. As you had to load from an elevator onto your shoulder, the bits got under your overalls and were smelly with a sweet pungent odour and made you itch like hell. On the way back to the yard after making a couple of deliveries to the local farms I passed, coming the other way, three of the McCains lorries including my Guy Big J. They all flashed and waved, but what made matters worse was that all three drivers had previously been employed at Fishers and they knew what a bloody horrible job sugar beet pulp was. I wept to myself – what a fool I am.

When not busy with Dale's or farm work I was sent to load through Central Haulage in Hull. This was only a small office clearing house and I knew the work was third hand anyway, but at least it got me away to do what I was best at. As always I tried to load into the London area where I knew from Fred's days I could always find a back load. A good source was to load reels of paper from Tilbury docks back to Hull and the Daily Mail warehouse there. Good work, good rates, and delivery time was for the following morning so I would park up in Hull and catch the train home and, of course, legally book a night out. Pete Fisher didn't like this and in his book I was fiddling a night out on expenses. I tried on a few occasions to explain that as long as the lorry was parked and I had noted on my records where it was parked, then what I did in my own time was my business. He didn't like that so, to say the least, we didn't get on.

Finally, after six or seven months it came to a head and he called me into his office. As I walked in he got up and walked over to the door and locked it. Umm, I thought, this looks like it is going to get serious. However, he was quite rational and we had a sensible although disagreeable discussion, in which he admitted that on the general haulage side I knew more and had better contacts than him and I should get my own lorry. We agreed I would leave that weekend. Sound advice for the years to come. Peter Fisher was eventually taken over by Dale Electric and was known as Fisher Dale Haulage Ltd. Pete Fisher was, I believe, employed by Dale's as the transport manager.

After leaving Fisher's, actually the following week, I started driving for Slaters Transport, part of the Tilcon Group based on the outskirts of Pickering, driving a Foden 150 Gardner engine artic, with the obligatory twelve-speed epicycle gear change. Their work was for the most part containers for Meri Line at South Bank, Middlesbrough, Whitby docks with timber and steel imported from the continent and fabricated steel from Wards of Sherburn and Skinningrove. Most of the trailers were Trombone trailers, where they would, by re-adjusting the locking pins, extend to sixty feet or more. Skinningrove also produced mine-arches, which would support the tunnels in coal mines. This was really a very good job and deliveries were all over the UK. The management were excellent and so long as you did the job they left you alone. Most of the drivers had been there for years, so were very protective of how the job should be done – nothing wrong with that and I got on well with the majority.

As I always hankered for long-distance work and, once the management realised I could find my own back loads, they were quite happy to let me loose. The only problem here was that every day they had a policy of pinning up in the drivers' room a wall chart of what every driver and lorry was doing. So a couple of the older hands, when they saw 'Read London-Scotland' et cetera, thought I was treated better than them; even though they didn't particularly want to do it and preferred more local work. The age-old scenario – just something to moan about. But they were, nevertheless, a good bunch of guys.

On a trip to South Wales, while driving on the A38 road near Burton on Trent, I noticed a chain had come loose on the load of steel I was carrying. I stopped in a lay-by, climbed on the back of the trailer, re-adjusted the tension and pulled down hard on the sylvester (a device where you hook both parts of the chain together). As I did so the chain snapped and I went over the side onto the main road, hitting my back as I fell on the chock rail of my trailer. Hell that hurt and I cursed my luck and misfortune, but got back on to the trailer and secured the load. By the time I got to South Wales I could hardly move (no air-ride seats then just a box-type seat). Somehow or other I unloaded then rang Morris the traffic manager, a great guy, and told him what had happened and how I felt. "Can you make it back home, Barry?" I said I could and reluctantly made my way back to the yard. As ever I hated the thought of a lorry running empty.

Back home, after a quick visit to my doctor, I was taken to Scarborough Hospital on Green Lane and admitted with a severe disc problem in my back and was put on traction for a solid three weeks. Not a pleasant experience at all. Sandra, in those days, didn't drive and Scarborough Hospital was difficult to get to, but she never missed a day without coming to see me, bless her.

While in hospital this guy, after hearing my reason for being there, mis-advised me that I should make an industrial accident claim against Slaters, as one of the doctors had told me I wouldn't be able to drive a lorry again; the only thing I could and wanted to do. So I did, which was a really big mistake, as I hadn't a hope in hell of being successful. Bear in mind I had a wife, two kids, a mortgage and no money saved; things looked pretty grim. So with only a minimum sick/accident payment each week, what could I do? My solicitor (who I know now was useless) told me I couldn't go back to Slaters while my claim was pending. So I went along to Boddy's Coaches, who had their garage at the end of our road and, after a bit of tuition, I passed my PSV bus drivers' test.

I really enjoyed this and although they didn't travel far afield the trips were quite varied. I would, when doing a mystery trip, smile to myself as the passengers would seem so excited not knowing where they were going, which was probably only a forty or fifty mile round trip with a teatime stopover. Boddy's Coaches also had another business and the name was so apt – Boddy and Son, Funeral Directors. Great!

Scanning the Hull Daily Mail job sections, I came across an advert for a continental coach driver. Immediately I was aroused at the prospect and Sandra urged me to follow it up, which the following morning I did. I rang up for an interview and later the same day I arrived at their office on The Land of Green Ginger. I met Lorraine and after a short interview was offered a job as a PSV driver going out that weekend to Yugoslavia. Where the hell is Yugoslavia, I thought but, undeterred, I eagerly accepted and she gave me all the literature about the company and told me to report back at 8 a.m. on Saturday morning. From here we would go to Dover and then onwards to Yugoslavia with a full load of passengers. So began my time with Halcyon Continental as a coach driver.

Somehow or other I managed to get a short term passport (which wasn't valid for Yugoslavia anyway!). On Saturday morning I caught the first train from Bridlington to Hull, which was inevitably late, so by the time I got to the Halcyon offices Lorraine had gone. What the hell, I caught the train to London Kings Cross, a bus to Victoria and a train to Dover, where I walked to Dover eastern docks and stood outside. Looking back, at the time it was a bit like finding a needle in a haystack; I didn't know what a Halcyon coach looked like, didn't know the time of the sailing, and hadn't a clue as to how I would get back home as I had almost run out of money, having spent what I had on getting to Dover. I was beginning to question my sanity.

When this coach approached, stood in the passenger side front window was Lorraine. She looked at me aghast and, I found out later, couldn't quite believe it was me stood there waiting for them. Having explained what had happened and that I had no money left, she readily made amends – one, if not the only, time a woman has given me money. As it turned out the coach was hired from Carnel's of Sheffield and the driver employed by them did have some limited experience of continental driving, so at least we found our way out of Calais okay. With two drivers, me included, we made our way via the autoroute through Paris, Lyons, Chambery, Susa (the Italian border), Torino, Milano and Trieste before crossing the border into Yugoslavia.

We then arrived at the campsite at Krajrevice to be met by a quite hostile band of campers. Bearing in mind this was now Monday morning and neither Peter (the other driver) nor I had slept since leaving home on the previous Saturday morning, apart from catnapping while the other drove. So we were both pretty well shot and could have done without this reception. What had happened was that they should have been picked up on the previous Saturday and should by now be back home, but the coach, on its way from Greece, had had an accident in Belgrade – quite a bad one – and had been impounded and the two drivers arrested and jailed. The passengers had been taken to a hotel awaiting rescue. Seemingly, under Yugoslavian law (Tito being very much in power) if any foreign driver had an accident without doubt it was their fault, as if they hadn't been in the country the accident wouldn't have taken place. Some kind of logic!

Russell Derry, the owner of Halcyon, was on his way to Belgrade to sort it out. Meanwhile the campers were adamant we should turn round and take them home. The situation was made worse as the would-be campers we had brought down looked very concerned as everything appeared so chaotic. Finally I was able to calm them down, explaining that we were both shattered and after a day's rest we would set off for home early the next morning. This seemed to work and we all made the best of the very limited space there was, as the site was way beyond capacity. However, our prior instructions were that we (Peter and I) had to go empty to Belgrade and pick up the accident coach and the two drivers involved, who had now lost it and refused to drive again. So, during the early hours of the morning we sneaked out of the campsite and drove to Belgrade Police Station where the arrested drivers and damaged coach were.

A more sorry sight I hadn't seen. Both were completely dishevelled and fatigued. They had been tried by something of a kangaroo court, but because of the circumstances leading up to the accident had got away lightly, as I found out much later. Some drivers who were involved in accidents were simply locked up and left. When we recovered the coach from the compound it was badly damaged on the rear end and the nearside, so some makeshift repairs were made. The remaining passengers were transferred to the Carnel's coach and my job was to drive the damaged coach.

When we eventually arrived back at the campsite in Krajrevice we were met by a very angry crowd of campers; rightly so as there weren't enough tents to accommodate them all. In the meantime, while we were in Belgrade, a few of the campers had notified the News of the World newspaper of their dilemma, which had in turn contacted not only their local papers but also the Hull Daily Mail, which ran a front page editorial which, although not the true saga, still slighted Halcyon Coaches.

Although the drive back to Calais was not without concern, as our route back was over Mont Cenis with its very steep climb and severe hairpin bends, the journey went reasonably well. On arrival back at Dover eastern docks, we were met by reporters who took photos of the coach. I declined to comment, but a few of the passengers made statements which I believe they used to claim damages against Halcyon. Whether or not they ever got anything I never knew.

Anyway, not deterred by this, my next trip only a couple of days later was to Athens in Greece. Dropping off passengers at Krajrevice, which was a lovely place, then on to Athens via Zagreb and Belgrade on the notorious accident A3 to E70 road. Then on to Nis and Skopia, eventually crossing the border at Geugelija into Greece. What a transformation, from the drab countryside of Yugoslavia. A big sign in English which read 'Welcome to Greece' was my first impression.

On production of the manifest of the passenger names and passport numbers the barrier was lifted and we had a beautiful drive through the valley of The Festival of Diana, down through the beach town of Larisa, after Thessalonika, and Lamia right on the beautiful blue seas of the Aegean, before dropping the remaining passengers near to the central station in Athens. After an overnight stay at Sisses-Camp Ambe, we picked up the previous week's passengers and trans-routed our way back to Krajrevice to pick up more passengers, then set off for Calais. Unfortunately, not far into our journey there was a loud bang – a rear tyre had blown out. We changed to the spare without a problem, but a couple of hours later we had another blowout; and quite a bit of unrest among our passengers. As we didn't have enough running money to get us home and buy a new tyre as well, a whip-round and another tyre, with great difficulty, was sought, bought and fitted.

All went well until we got to Tournes in France, then 'Bang!' and another tyre blowout. Now there was panic among the passengers and they refused to go any further. One of them made off and telephoned the British Embassy in Lyons. Eventually two representatives from the embassy arrived, set up a green baize-type table alongside our coach, took notes and asked for those who wanted to be repatriated back to the UK. Without hesitation most of them did; I was kinda tempted myself.

We were parked quite near the railway station and the mainline train from Marseille to Paris, which seemingly didn't have a scheduled stop at Tournes, was stopped and our one-time passengers boarded and then they were gone. We contacted Lorraine in the Hull office and eventually some money was transferred to us so that we could buy another tyre, with enough money left over to get us home.

Another regular trip was to Mungo Beach near L'Escala, Gerona in Spain. This was a doddle: leave Calais Saturday afternoon, arrive Sunday lunchtime, leaving the following Friday lunchtime. Time to relax and enjoy the sunshine, which I certainly did.

As my claim against Slaters was going nowhere, just the wrong way, I had to make a decision about what I was going to do as the season with Halcyon was coming to a close. The coach that had been in Belgrade had by now been repaired, so I went to pick it up from Plaxtons in Cayton near Scarborough. By chance I met George, one of Pete Fisher's drivers. He told me they were doing some work pulling trailers for MAT Transport Ltd, based in Hull, on UK work, but their own trucks were running to Italy. My interest was piqued. Probably, apart from the experience I gained at Halcyon, the best thing was to meet my lifelong friend Chris Teal, who as well as driving for them was their fitter and mechanic. Chris was brilliant; he kept all the coaches running. One, a Bristol coach, was renowned for engine seizures and Chris on many occasions was known to fit a new one at the side of the road in some outlying foreign location. A great guy and I have the privilege of being his son Oliver's godfather.

So I left Halcyon on extremely good terms. Russell Derry told me I could have a job full-time anytime with them, and in the following years I took advantage of this for short-term holiday working breaks.

Me in my Halcyon coach driving days.

Me and another driver for Halcyon Coaches.

Chapter Six

After meeting George from Fisher's I rang MAT Transport in Hull enquiring about a vacancy and spoke to the manager, Mr Cliff Leader, who invited me for an interview. When I arrived at the depot on Popple Street in Hull I discovered that Cliff Leader had been a driver, who I did recognise, for Bowker Transport based in Blackburn and we had shared on a regular basis the same transport digs (Ma Smith's) in Wood Green, London. I had a driving test in my first ever Scania 110 with a synchromesh gearbox and I was told by their fitter, Dave Clark, not to double de-clutch; certainly a first as all my previous lorries had crash box gears. All seemed to go well and I was offered a job as a UK-Continental driver. I was overjoyed and couldn't wait to start, which was in two weeks time. I went back to Slaters, handed in my notice and finished that weekend. A Blackpool-Lakes weekend for Halcyon, taking Sandra and Kevin with me and some forty or so passengers, fitted in ideally.

The first lorry allocated to me at MAT was YYO 458H, fleet number MAT1, a gorgeous blue Scania 110. This had a full length couchette bed that was housed behind the driver-passenger seat that let down once the backs had been taken off. How quiet and powerful they drove after the likes of noisy Gardner engines. I loved the work on and off the docks, picking up trailers from Jansen & Meyer, a MAT subsidiary company based in Holland.

My first trip to France was loading from Bradford to Le Havre with two digger machines, shipping from Southampton to Le Havre via Seagull Ferries on a converted freighter which was pretty awful and pitched and rolled with the slightest movement at sea. Not being a good sailor I was feeling pretty grim. After customs clearance and delivery of the diggers, I then drove to Vierzon via Rouen, Chartres and Orleans to spend the night there. The following morning the manager of Case Tractors, who spoke English with an American accent, took control and I was loaded with two JCB type tractors, cleared customs on site and drove back to Le Havre for the night crossing ferry. The following day I was back up to Bradford to unload; a really good, enjoyable job which took from leaving on the Sunday to returning back to Hull on the Wednesday. This was a weekly job and I did quite a few of them. Cawthorne and Sinclair's from Birtley, Co. Durham had an office in Le Havre and they did the export work for Caterpillar. I got to know one of their drivers quite well, who was the father of Brian Robson, who became the Manchester United and England football captain.

Eventually I loaded from ICI's warehouse in Heywood, Lancashire for Italy and on the Sunday left Hull for Dover western docks. After completing customs, which required a TIR Carnet (this was the recognised customs document long before we entered the EEC), I shipped to Dunkerque and drove to the south of Paris on the A6 autoroute and parked up at the services – a long day. From there to Macon in the south, calling at Jacques Borel autostop, Nantua, eventually to the Mont Blanc tunnel. Customs formalities for onward travel into Italy were chaotic at the compound once through the tunnel, as traffic converged erratically and drivers pushed and shoved to get their documents stamped by both the French and Italian customs. Once completed, which could take anything from two to four hours, I drove to Concorrezzo, east of Milano to the customs clearance compound. My first sighting of this was the forwarding agents walking around arm in arm, one holding a brolly in the pouring rain while the other had masses of papers and the carnets in his arms. Clearance took all day which was regular and normal. By 6 p.m. I was cleared and a van and driver escorted me to, I think, six or seven drops, all within the Monza area. By 9 p.m. I was empty and it was time for something to eat and drink. The restaurant at Concorrezzo was a bustling hive of activity and served excellent food.

Our agent for backwarding was Mario at Gottardo Ruffoni in Via Toffette, south of Milano. From there, anywhere within the area, we made collections; sometimes a bit annoying as what you had picked up was trans-shipped onto other trucks and vice versa, never leaving their depot. After clearing, and before 10 p.m., the main aim was to be over Mont Blanc to park up at Bonneville in France; a few hours sleep, a quick visit to Switzerland for cigars, chocolates, et cetera and then to Dunkerque. The ferry from Dover-Dunkerque-Dover was also the route for the boat-train passenger service, which at all times had priority, and many times your truck would be looking into the sea hanging from the rear of the boat.

One of the best jobs MAT had was loading reels of paper from Scotland to Naples and the Pirelli tyre factory; for some reason they covered the new tyres in paper. On one of these trips I escorted Colin Peart who hadn't been to Italy before. After delivery, making our way back to Milano, we parked up in the mountains for the night. It was freezing cold and we had to use the cold starts the following morning. Colin's truck lost most of its power, so I stayed with him back to Milano, which seemed to take forever. I had been told to leave him but I refused, and consequently became weekended. Cliff Leader was fuming with me and I was told I would be reprimanded once back home. The problem with Colin's truck was that the cold start had stuck in, but as soon as this was released all was fine and we got back to the UK trouble free. I had to go into Cliff's office for a supposed dressing-down, but he had cooled off by then. One thing in my favour was that Brian Yeardly was then the Junior Transport Co-ordinator and he was at that time lodging at Colin Peart's house, so I am sure he got matters sorted before we got back home. Brian Yeardly, as we all know, became and still is the Super-cube low-rider international haulier in these parts. To me, a true professional.

Eventually I got a brand new Scania 110 (reg. no. GRH 233L) and had this for a couple of years or so, before I was sacked. Prior to this happening MAT had moved to a brand new depot on Dairycoates Industrial Estate on Brighton Street in Hull; a super, purpose-built depot. In doing so, I believe the personal touch was lost. However, on this particular day I had been shunting containers on and off the dock in Hull. By the end of the day my instructions were given for the following day. I had used the same skeleton trailer all that day and it was MAT policy to check wheel studs every time you picked up a trailer and every morning before setting off, as some trailers, especially the Jansen & Mayer trailers, had a bad habit of wheels coming loose. Anyway, I checked my trailer studs before going home for the night. At 6 a.m. the following morning, noting that my lorry hadn't moved from where I had parked it the night before, I took a quick look round and set off. In those days the M62 wasn't built and the main road west was the A63. At Slipper Bridge, near Gilberdyke, I lost the two rear wheels off the tandem trailer. As I was empty, apart from the empty container on board, I didn't feel or notice anything wrong. I stopped at the Woodside Cafe near Goole looking forward to a hearty breakfast, only to see the two wheels missing.

I dropped the trailer and went back in search of the wheels but could find only one, which with the help of another driver we lifted onto my tractor chassis. I rang the office to tell them of my dilemma. Tug Wilson, whom I had known from my Valley Transport days, said, "Barry, did you check your wheel studs this morning?" I replied that I had last night before I left. "Well," said Tug, "you know MAT policy. You must check every morning." Eventually, back at the depot, I was called into the office. Previously another driver, Jock Cairns from Scarborough, had been sacked for losing his trailer wheels. A new transport manager had just been appointed and I explained what had happened. He said, "I'm not sure what to do here." I told him he had no option other than to sack me, which he did. I am my own worst critic, and I had broken the rules, so I had to go.

The police were involved as the wheel I couldn't find had hit a lorry coming the other way. Although there were no injuries to anyone, a bit of damage had been done. I made a statement, but as far as I am aware nothing came of it. Days later, I saw the same officer in Bridlington, just by chance, and he was sympathetic that I had been sacked. Although, about a year later Cliff Leader rang and asked me to go back. I declined and my MAT Transport driving days were over. Although MAT played a big part in my later working life.

Me with YYO 438H on NS Ferries freighter. Note the narrow cab - no sleeper cab, only a couchette and two weeks away from home.

Me with Kevin somewhere in Italy for MAT Transport.

Dinner break parked up for the weekend in Naples, Italy.

Delivering groupage near Ulm, Austria.

Me with same brand new unit GRH 233L and Jansen & Meyer trailer.

Chapter Seven

Out of work with time to gather my thoughts, my initial intention was to find a job running to the Middle East. Due to the long delays in the port of Jedda, the whole of the Middle East was fast developing and there was a call for European-made goods which were widely sought after. This opened up the doors for overland routes to expand and the whole Middle East continent was booming. Various companies specialised in this trade and the opportunities were vast. Then, out of the blue, I became aware that the Satra Motor Co. was opening a pre-delivery inspection (PDI) factory on Carnaby Industrial Estate, importing the Russian-built Moskvitch cars. They were shipped into Hull before their PDI and then onwards delivered to their appointed dealers throughout the UK. Initially, Theakstons of Driffield had partly been involved building the factory. In turn, they got the job of bringing the cars in from King George Dock in Hull to Carnaby.

The trucks, which they must have dug up from a scrap yard, were reinstated and somehow made ready for the job in hand. I was employed on a temporary basis and given some tuition on how to operate the truck when loading the cars on to the top and bottom decks. At first it was quite alarming as you had to reverse the first car onto the top deck thinking you were literally driving into open space. The Moskvitch cars were noted as non-starters and to get them going was quite a task. Most of them had little or no fuel in them and petrol had to be sought by whatever means. Four loads of five cars per truck was the expectation, but quite often this could not be achieved because of the problems starting the cars.

Behind the scenes Lathams from Preston had secured the contract with Satra and very soon I was introduced to Mr Jack Ward for an interview as a regular driver employed by Lathams. Mr Ward was a gentleman, a lovely man with a great deal of experience in the car transport industry. He was based and lived in Ipswich and was the General Distribution Manager for Volvo, employed by Lathams, and would look after both Volvo and Satra contracts. Mr Ward offered me a job straight away and outlined the wages, bonuses et cetera – fantastic mileage, bonus, backload incentives, all in all the very best payment package I had ever been offered. Mr Ward asked me to go in my own car to Preston (expenses paid) and pick up my designated vehicle and then put my own car on the back of my new truck to come back to Carnaby. I met both Mr Michael and Mr Martin Latham at the Preston depot – both lovely guys – and they welcomed me to the company.

The truck allocated to me was a five-car lorry and trailer (three on the lorry and two on the trailer), a Guy Big J with a 120 Gardner engine, painted in the livery of Lathams, a darkish blue colour. It looked very nice, but if you had a head wind you'd probably go faster backwards. Back to Carnaby with my car on board; my first day with Lathams.

Next morning my first load was a multi-drop around the West Riding area. With some trepidation I loaded up, but the procedure was quite different from the seven-car artic of Theakstons, as ramps taking you from the flat trailer onto the static running ramps onto the lorry meant literally driving over an empty space with nothing to stop you going over the side – a bit harrowing at first. Kevin came for a ride out with me, and Alan Parker, who had in the meantime also been employed that very day, followed me for quite a distance to make sure no cars fell off, then made his way to Preston to pick up his truck, as I had previously done.

All went reasonably well until my last drop when I drove off the ramps with the front wheel and ended up completely lopsided and unable to move. Thankfully the garage owner was very sympathetic and by jacking up the car we got it back onto the ramps with no damage, resulting in a 'clear' signature; very lucky Barry, as most dealers would have signed as 'damaged'. Back to the yard, loaded up for the next day and I felt quite satisfied I was with Lathams.

Apart from the best wage packet I had ever earned, the job itself was excellent and deliveries took you to all parts of the UK. Though I can't say I was impressed with the five-car road train as, apart from the lack of any power, it was awkward to drive. One

52

really good job I had was to take some show cars to a hotel just off Park lane in London's West End, where a press and dealer launch took place. I was treated extremely well, more as a guest that just a driver. This was a three-day event and I never moved from the hotel grounds.

By then Satra had taken on the franchise for Lada cars, basically a Fiat built under licence in Russia but sporting a Lada badge. It was a vast improvement on the Moskvitch, which really didn't take off in the UK, but at least it got a foothold in the UK for Satra.

Eventually I was given a Big J Guy, seven-car transporter with a 150 Gardner engine, which was a big improvement, although still a bit under powered. Although I didn't want it I was voted by the other drivers and yard staff to be their union shop steward. Not for me really as I certainly wasn't militant enough and couldn't understand what there was to moan about or improve on with the job at Lathams. One of the yard staff took objection to my indifference to his moans and took a swing at me – wrong thing for him to do – so I retaliated and laid him out. Wrong thing for me to do, as I thought I would lose my job for fighting. Mr Ward had no alternative other than to reprimand me, but in my defence other staff had witnessed the event and that the other guy had started it. I was given a verbal warning while the other guy was sacked, as he did have an attitude problem.

While I was shop steward, Lathams was bought out by Cartransport, whose main office was based in Leamington Spa. As shop steward I had to attend several meetings regarding procedure, wage structure, et cetera. Basically it was a bit of a jolly, a day out, all paid for.

The job did change for the better, as being part of a much bigger concern backloading, which paid a premium to us drivers, boosted our earnings significantly. Vehicle servicing and repairs was allocated to the old B.R.S. depot in Goole, which again was an advantage.

Ladas had by now proved quite a popular car to buy with the general public and deliveries to the appointed dealers covered the whole of the UK, and with the added bonus of backloading I had never earned such wages. One of the best backloads was from Ramsgate in Kent, where we loaded VW cars and the brilliant VW camper vans, which we used as sleeping quarters; a bonus in itself as you could fully stretch out, not like being cramped up laid across in the bonnet of your truck.

Eventually, after quite some negotiating, I was allocated a 19.24 Mercedes single-bunk sleeper truck; what a difference, a real bonus. But, no matter how good the job and the excellent wage structure were, the thoughts of driving back to the continent tugged at me.

Quite by chance I saw an advert in the Hull Daily Mail that Hull Ships Stores were looking for a transport manager to head up their new venture into delivering ships stores on to the continent with two-man road trains. Immediately my interest was aroused, so I made an appointment with the owner, Mr Alan Taylor, although I had no interest whatsoever in being the manager, rather my thoughts stretched way beyond and I was only interested in driving one of these new trucks.

Mr Taylor and I seemed to get on very well and he, quite rightly, said that whoever got the job as manager would employ his chosen drivers, but that he would give him my details. By chance (and I can't recall his name) a guy from MAT Transport got the job. He knew me and contacted me to say I was definitely a candidate as a driver. As far as I am aware he was too valuable an asset to MAT Transport and they head-hunted him back to them by promoting him to their London office.

Mr Taylor contacted me and offered me the job as Driver Co-ordinator; I later found out I had been highly recommended by the guy whose name I can't recall. So with some deliberations and the OK from Sandra I handed in my notice to Mr Ward. He was very surprised but wished me well – what a lovely guy. My last week there was spent training Roy Smith who has become one of my best friends.

So my days as a car transporter driver were over. I really enjoyed my time there, certainly earned excellent wages and to some extent was able to enjoy a family social life. Barry, again, what have you done? Will you ever be satisfied?

Me with the first Ford Trans-continental for Hull Ships Stores somewhere in France.

Chapter Eight

So, here I was employed by Hull Ships Stores, based in an ancient style, quayside warehouse adjacent to the River Hull, packed to overflowing with goods of every description, while the top floor was laden, like an Aladdin's cave, with tools, spares et cetera. It even had the old style outside pulley for lifting heavy gear to the top floor. Mr Taylor senior, who played a very active part, was quite a character and, with the greatest of respect, could easily pass as 'Steptoe'. His midday sandwich was wrapped in what looked to be soiled greaseproof paper – ugh! Nevertheless, a very astute gentleman.

My first shock, quickly followed by the second, was my wages – £46.00 less stoppages. A far cry from the £350-£400 at Cartransport. Sandra certainly didn't relish that. The second was that the two lorry road trains were way behind production as the bodies were being specially built for purpose. So for at least two months I travelled backwards and forwards to Hull at my own expenses and basically just helped in the warehouse. This was costing me not only money we had saved, but was boring me rigid. I was seriously contemplating trying for my job back at Cartransport.

Then all of a sudden a ships stores load came up to go to Bari in Italy. I organised a Man tractor unit and fridge trailer from Graylease and loaded up frozen goods, separated by a makeshift wall from the deck and engine, and bonded goods et cetera. With what seemed like a mountain of customs-related paperwork, the trailer was customs-sealed down to the North Sea ferries ship out to Zeebrugge and I was on my way.

Following the route I had travelled many times before with MAT Transport en route for Italy, I reached the junction at Chamonix before climbing the ascent up to the Mont Blanc tunnel. There, as always, were the Gendarmes who stopped trucks at random to inspect their T-forms, before proceeding up the mountain to the tunnel entrance. Unfortunately my T-forms (the official customs document), which ordinarily described the goods carried, just showed 'As per attached manifest'. On his inspection he discovered I had on board matches and a barrel of paraffin – obviously a hazard in his eyes – and he immediately parked me up for the whole weekend, making me buy flashing roof-mounted lights and hazard boards, and barring me from travelling through Mont Blanc.

On Sunday night my documents were returned to me and I had to re-route via Ventimiglia – a hell of a way round. Finally, I arrived in Bari in the early hours of the Tuesday morning absolutely shattered, but still in time for the ship's arrival. The ironical part to this bit of the saga was that because the ship was anchored way out in the bay, all the stores were loaded onto an open-top barge, pulled by a launch, where I sat with the pilot. Half way out to the ship a squall blew up, the barge heaved to one side and overboard went the 40-foot gangway I had brought over in my truck. There was no way it could be retrieved and it was lost. The rest of the stores, however, were unloaded with no further problems. For a backload I contacted Mario, who was still with Gottardo Ruffonis in Milano, who loaded me back to the UK. As I recall no further mishaps occurred on the way back.

Still, the two road trains were not ready for delivery, so I kept the Graylease rented truck and trailer and found work with S.T.L. Transport working from McCains. S.T.L. was formed as an independent company from the now defunct Humber-McVeigh with a new depot in Cayton. At least by doing this I wasn't reliant on working in the HSS warehouse.

Eventually the two road trains arrived and, to be honest, they proved unworkable: the lorry, a Man 232, was underpowered and it had a fridge-controlled loading bay with a heavy tail-lift and side door; and the four-axle trailer was a simple dry-boxed trailer with king locks. The whole outfit could only operate at twenty-eight tons gross – just not practical – and of course any item longer that twenty feet wouldn't fit inside, but from a non-professional viewpoint they at least looked good.

By now HSS had increased its workforce. John Williamson (better known as Jesus) and I helped two of my former workmates from Fred Wright's, Bobby Brown and Dave Booker, to get jobs. HSS also moved to new premises on Spyvee Street, which included a purpose-built warehouse and cold store and a bonded store on site. The official opening of the warehouse was overseen by John Prescott who was the Labour candidate for East Hull, and later became the Deputy Prime Minister. Both Sandra and I had the dubious honour of shaking hands with him, which I can only liken to a wet-lettuce gesture.

HSS bought from Tates of Leeds two Ford transcontinental tractor units with Cummins engines. The transcon was a whole new concept with a cab module, similar to a French-built Berliet, housed over the engine and chassis. A really gorgeous looking truck, they would literally fly and could reach 100 miles per hour; the only problem was trying to stop them, as the braking was diabolical because the brake shoes were wedge shaped and prone to glazing. I repeatedly took mine back to Tates whose only solution was to rough up the shoes and to inform me that my driving technique was not severe enough – hmm! But I loved this truck and went all over the continent with it delivering ships stores to such places as Piraeus in Greece, Cadiz in Spain and Gdynia in Poland, always with admiring, inquisitive notice from other drivers.

By now HSS was getting quite busy, so they bought three Man V10 tractor units in addition to the present fleet, and destinations for ships stores went far and wide. On one of my trips to Italy just about everything went wrong: the makeshift wall in the fridge that separated the frozen from the dry goods fell down while en route and consequently froze even the bonded goods. I reloaded peaches from near Ravenna for Spitalfields and Covent Garden in London and while en route the fridge unit controlling the cool temperature broke down. Repeated efforts to make makeshift repairs were in vain; a Petter agent, when I eventually found one, just wasn't interested. A bit of a low time and my only solution was to get back to the UK in more or less one hit and get unloaded ASAP.

On the way I stopped for an evening meal at The Bakehouse in St Cyr, a place I knew well, that served excellent fare and was popular with all European truckers. While there a TV crew was filming a journey of an owner/driver from the UK to Trieste in Italy, highlighting the tricks, if not unscrupulous methods some drivers took. I played only a very small part where I was filmed eating a hearty meal and responding to some passing remark. This was eventually shown as a TV documentary called 'A Run For Your Money', and I think I still have the video I bought.

Eventually, absolutely knackered having had no sleep, I arrived at the New Covent Garden on Nine Elms Lane in London. Because I was a day and a bit early, the importer told me I had to wait until the following day to unload. In desperation, or stupidity (not sure which), I told him of my fridge problem, which was met by, "I couldn't care less. You can dump them in the Thames for me mate." Great! Anyway he did relent and did unload me. Although the peaches seemed okay an endorsement was made on my CMR about the fridge, but as far as I am aware no claim ever arose.

While this whole event was taking place my train of thought was, if I can sort this out for someone else while only paid as an employee, I can most certainly do it for myself. Various ways of achieving this came to mind; funny how the mind can run away with you when on the long journey home.

Chapter Nine
My route to being an owner/driver

In Bridlington the fishing fleet was more or less run by two companies – G Bogg Ltd and Thomas Hamlins Ltd – where they set up skippers with a 50% share in their boats, and at that time the fishing industry was extremely lucrative. Consequently the skippers and crew were quite affluent. So, I thought, if that works why not involve them in transport on an owner/driver basis. Through a very good friend of ours, Jim Scotter, I was introduced to Mr Jonathan Watson Hall, the M.D. of Thomas Hamlins Ltd. I can only say that I sold my idea to him and he agreed in principle.

I already held, through grandfather rights, my CPC (Certificate of Professional Competence) so I applied for an operator's licence for two articulated lorries and trailers. This was quite involved: advertising in the local paper to see if there were any objectors; and finding an operating centre. With the approval of an ex-MAT Transport manager, Brian Lill, who now worked for Bowker Transport based on Victoria Dock in Hull, he promised me work, so from an operating point of view all seemed OK. Now for the financial part. Mr J W Hall introduced me to the manager at Westminster Bank where, against repossession of our house at 21 East Road, I was able to secure a loan of £15,000 – a heart-stopping sum of money. Sandra was in full agreement, but 'Wow' what a decision.

A lot of thought went into what unit I would buy: first choice a Scania would have been fantastic, but exceeded my funds. So without doubt the best to meet my budget was a DAF 2800 DKS, four by two. And again without doubt the best supplier was Thompsons of Beverley, the main DAF dealership, and they were excellent.

A couple of months went by and all seemed to be going well. At this point I loaded ships stores, while still employed at HSS, for a ship in Piraeus, Athens in Greece, which was normally a three-week round trip. I went to Mr Taylor, the M.D. at HSS, and told him that when I got back I would be leaving to set up as an owner/driver. He looked surprised but said very little. Collecting all the relevant paperwork, TIR Carnet, Carnet de Passage, et cetera, off I went to the N.S.F. terminal and shipped out that night from Hull to Zeebrugge.

By now, I had made a few trips to Greece with relatively few problems, but this trip was not as normal in that it was to the Greek island of Siros, to the dockyard there. The ship *Upway Grange* was undergoing an extensive re-fit. En route and well into Greece I had to return to the Yugoslavian border as one of the other drivers, Angus Suttie, had problems with a permit, which I helped to sort out. Eventually I arrived in Piraeus, the port of Athens, from where the agent then directed me to the port of Rafina on the east coast for the ferry to Siros, a six and a half hour ferry journey.

On arrival I had a police escort to the shipyard as the streets were so narrow and not meant for a 32-ton juggernaut. The agent had booked and paid for a hotel room for me – to say the least it was authentic, but clean. The following day I was just waiting before finally delivering to the ship. Back on the ferry to Rafina I rang HSS but was told to ring again when I reached Thessalonika, which I did, only to be told to turn around and go back 160 miles to Patras and load near there in what turned out to be two days later. Although by now I was running out of money, I was able to pay 14,000 drachmas (about £230) and caught the ferry from Patras/Ancona and spent a very pleasant time on the Ionian Star. Finally, I had a good trip home with no problems.

Three weeks away and it was good to be going home; knowing that when I got back home my days with HSS as an employed driver were almost at an end and soon I would be an owner/driver with a lot more responsibility thrust upon me – could I make it work? While away on this trip my mind had been working overtime on the idea: would it be possible to work under the banner of HSS as an owner/driver, painted in their livery, which would not be totally legal, but I'd have access to doing ships stores throughout the continent. When I saw Mr Alan Taylor and suggested the idea he was in total agreement and was pleased at the idea. He said he didn't want to lose me – a statement not used too often about me!

Although I could ill afford it I took a couple of weeks off to prepare for the arrival of my new truck. Dave Nicholls helped me to build a brick-based shed in the back garden to store all the bits and pieces I would need to help me get started. We made a good job of it. The head salesman at Thompsons was Mr Arnold Worrell, a lovely guy totally dedicated to DAF trucks, and eventually I was told that my truck was at High Wycombe undergoing a PDI. Somehow I persuaded him that I wanted to collect it and no one else was to drive it. Silly really, as it had already been driven from the plant in Eindhoven to the ferry and from the ferry to High Wycombe. Anyway, Arnold took me down and there waiting for me was my beautiful DAF tractor unit. I had a lovely drive back to Beverley and was really excited about my new venture. Painting and sign-writing was undertaken by Stephensons in Hull and the sign-writer painted cross flags of the UK and France on each wing-guard. Looking good.

Soon I was on the road trading as B. B. Read & Co (with reg. no. VAG 37S) and was kept very busy, both on ships stores throughout the whole of Europe and, in between, working directly with McCains Foods in Scarborough delivering frozen chips to Kesteren in Holland, and with Seamer Transport. To begin with I used an HSS trailer but eventually I bought my own freight Bonallack tandem-axle trailer with a thermo king fridge (N4652) from Marshalls of Cambridge, painted and sign-written as B. B. Read & Co Bridlington. It looked great and I was doing well.

Pretty soon I thought I saw an opportunity to buy another DAF unit (BRH 750T) and I gave this to a prospective owner/driver, Trevor, who had previously worked at Ash Grove, the MAN agents, as a fitter. Unfortunately, he was a good fitter but couldn't handle being a driver; long days, nights out, just what drivers have to put up with.

Thursday 15th February 1979.

Two days before, I had collected a brand new fridge trailer from Graylease and loaded ships stores for Antwerp. At that time Hull dockers were on strike, so as I shipped out on the night of the 15th aboard N.S.F. Norwind, the previous night's unaccompanied trailers were still on board. The weather was atrocious, a force-10 gale was blowing, and very soon the Norwind was heaving and leaning heavily to one side. The purser, Olaf, said it was his worst night in twenty-seven years at sea. Unfortunately, a Bowker trailer loaded with chipboard broke free and overturned onto my lorry and trailer causing severe damage.

Normally the ferry would dock in Zeebrugge at 9 a.m., but it was 19:00 hours that day before we finally docked. The loading deck was littered with smashed up lorries and trailers. For two days the ship's hold was a total mess before it was finally cleared. I found that my unit had a twisted chassis and a badly damaged cab. VAG 37S was finally taken to a supposed specialist in Dewsbury where it stayed for about a month before I agreed to take it back, as the nearside front was leaning. All in all this set me back and I felt very much, what am I doing here?

Mr Alan Taylor at HSS was very good to me and I worked in the office organising the transport, but I needed to be back on the road. So I hired a Volvo unit from Graylease and did a ships stores job to Marseille. At least while I was off the road it did give me time to try and sort out my insurance, as the ferry companies have exemption for claims due to weather.

Another big problem that was looming was Trevor. Early the next morning in Grimsby, he refused to load a cargo of fish for Boulogne from Alan Glaves, so we had a big argument and he left. This took place at about 20:00 hours and he had the keys for BRH 750T in Beverley. As a matter of chance I rang Alan Parker to see if he could take me to Beverley to collect the keys. Alan had just been found out about his affair and he was only too willing to take me. All went okay with the load to Boulogne and Paris and I reloaded back from Holland to the UK. A guy from Stockport bought BRH 750T for £17,750 and although quite apprehensive about the cheque being cleared, it eventually was. A lesson I learned for future reference.

Finally I got my DAF unit (VAG 37S) back, although the cab was still leaning, but between Thompsons and myself we rectified the problem. We did this by putting shims under the front nearside spring to level it up. It worked but I was always aware of it. Nevertheless it was good to be back working with VAG 37S.

HSS were now in their heyday and busy with ships stores to the continent, so I had plenty of work on. A fairly regular destination was a town called Le Ciotat, east of Marseilles, along with some stores to a company in Marseilles called Marsup, who were also ship chandlers, more or less just catering for local shipping. A nice feature of Le Ciotat was that the harbour was clean and ideal for swimming in after unloading. Roy Smith, who took my job at Cartransport, came with me once for a jolly. We enjoyed it, but one night in a bar in Marseilles we felt threatened by some guys from the French Foreign Legion and we beat a hasty retreat, not really knowing where we were heading after we had downed a few drinks.

Marsup did offer me the possibility of buying and transporting stores from the UK to them, which at a later date I did pursue, but what with the hassle and prior expense involved I thought better of it. Besides I would have been treading on HSS's toes and that I certainly didn't want to do; Mr Alan Taylor was always so good to me.

One of my favourite runs was to the Greek island of Siros. This entailed clearing at the notorious border crossing at Spielfeld-Sentils to join the long queue of trucks waiting for transit clearance into Yugoslavia. The Austrian customs, just as their German counterparts, were quick and efficient; not so the Yugoslavians. Anyway, four hours later I'm on my way through Maribor to Zagreb and Belgrade over the most atrocious road surfaces imaginable. Yugoslavia was a semi-communist country and everything looked so drab and dreary. Perhaps it was being in a truck, but it looked so much worse than when I had been coming through with a coach for Halcyon. Eventually I spotted a restaurant with loads of trucks parked outside. Later, after a few more trips I got to know this restaurant-cum-truckstop as 'The Trees'. One of the dubious attractions of this place was the so-called 'ladies of the night' who frequently sold their wares. But, hell, you really must be scraping the barrel to fancy any one of them, as they were so big and ugly and probably would be better placed behind or pulling a plough – gruesome.

From there I would then catch a ferry from the Greek mainland to the island. This was a bit like a bus service calling at other islands and took about four hours to get there. Because my fridge was too high for inside the ferry I had to let the tyres down a bit on the drive axle to lower the height. Also when arriving in Siros a police escort took me to the dockyard, as the only way to get there was all one way through the town, and going the wrong way. A hotel was usually provided by the agent at the shipping company's expense.

On one such trip Kevin, who was about thirteen years old, came with me; how he did this we both never knew. While waiting in a massive truck queue at Spielfeld on the Austrian Yugoslav border, he drove the lorry right up to the border post situated on a hill, much to my amazement and pleasure, not to mention saving about two to three hours waiting time. On the same trip, after a night out on the town with some of the ship's crew we were a bit worse for wear the following morning. We had been allocated the hospital beds on the ship only to be awakened by the clanging of the moorings as the ship was leaving to go to Algeria. A hasty disembarkation was made by Kevin and myself, but this was a later event as the lorry was my first Scania 141 (LAT 904V), which I bought in December 1979.

One of the jobs that HSS acquired was to load pizza cases from Tolona Pizzas in Skelmersdale, Lancashire to Oslo in Norway, travelling to Grimsby to catch either the MV Domino or Destro, of the Ellermen & Wilson line, leaving port on a Friday evening to arrive in Oslo late on the Sunday evening, after calling at other Scandinavian ports. Staying on board all the time, especially as no other, or only occasionally, passengers were on board, I found it quite boring and a waste of time, especially when passing Flamborough Head and seeing the lighthouse flashing. After customs clearance I would find my delivery point and unloading was always very good. On more than one occasion the snow and cold was a problem and I had to dig my way out.

Then it would be a drive to Holland and backload from there, as we had no German quota permits; except once when I loaded from Sweden with pork sides and caught the ferry back to Felixstowe and met Mats Erikson, who was also on the ferry and became a lifelong friend. I invited him to come and stay with us for the weekend and some time later his daughter Cecilia made friends with Joanne, my daughter, and she came to stay with us.

By the late seventies, early eighties, the various trade unions had such a stranglehold on the country that even the likes of rubbish collection, funerals, car manufacturing were being held to ransom by strikes. Although far from being in sympathy or holding any political views it was a difficult time and the Conservative government of the day, headed by the Prime Minister Maggie Thatcher, was hell-bent on breaking their power. Consequently shipping was very much on the agenda, where the crews of ocean-going merchant shipping was crewed by mainly British crew members, and as such were all union members. The ship owners retaliated by flagging out their ships under Panamanian flags, getting rid of the ordinary seaman and employing only those with officer status. Consequently the ships stores of English food produce floundered and HSS were faced with a dramatic decline in their continental chandlering business, when they were heavily involved in transport designed for shipping stores.

While this whole scenario was taking place, the Falklands war erupted, which gave some respite to HSS and we became heavily involved in refurbishing ships of all kinds to take their place in the conflict. Our main task was to take parts to Valetta in Malta to refurbish such vessels. We would load anywhere in the UK, drive via France and Italy and take the ferry from the port of Reggio-Calabra to Valetta, then drive in convoy to the dockyard there and return to reload whatever we could back to the UK.

66

The rewards for this were very lucrative and, like in previous wars, quite a few people capitalised and made huge sums of money, myself included, as we were paid on a round trip basis, plus whatever we found as a backload. One trip that stood out was when Alan Parker, one of my drivers, took a flat-bed trailer with a 12.5-foot wide load of steel plate all the way without an escort. Normally such a load would warrant an escort convoy but the exceptional Alan did this on his own without any problem, except for a fine from the Italian police without a receipt. Good on you Alan, well deserved. The *Norland*, the Hull-Europoort ferry was refurbished in Valetta and served with distinction as a troop carrier.

After the conflict ended HSS was flat and they tried to rely on ordinary road haulage. One day Mr Alan Taylor called me to his office and instructed me, in confidence, that he needed to reduce his fleet significantly, but needed cover for any continental ships stores jobs. He suggested I buy his three MAN V10 units and trailers to which I rapidly explained that I didn't have the finance for that kind of expenditure. I'm sure Mr Taylor, being the businessman he was, suggested that as long as one lorry every day was in the yard to take a ships stores job for whatever came up, he would pay me for that, and the other two I would pay him for on a weekly basis, but do whatever I wanted to do. In theory this sounded OK, and in practice was beneficial to both parties. My only stipulation was that the bilateral general quota permits HSS had gained over the years be transferred through the IRFF International Road Freight Office to me. This was agreed to and, as such, opened up a whole market to me, which in fairness was what I knew. General quota permits were on a very strict association and were a bilateral agreement on a like for like basis between France, Germany, Italy, Spain and beyond. Although the system was fragmented: whereas the French customs on your point of entry and departure nearly always insisted on your permit and stamped it accordingly, the UK customs didn't, so a total imbalance was created and UK hauliers were somewhat penalised. But, like everything, ways and means prevailed and a ten franc note worked wonders, but you were always in fear of running the gauntlet.

Diesel fuel in your tank was another ploy, especially by the French customs, where you had to declare the fuel you had on board, and anything above fifty litres you had to pay duty on as UK fuel at that time was much cheaper. Quite often they would dip your tank and fine you on top for the undeclared amount. When I was driving for MAT Transport we had a scam where the Scania 110s had a push-down ignition key and it would send your fuel gauge nearly to empty. This worked for a time until the customs officers got wise to it then there was a heavy fine for evasion.

Much later one of my drivers, Fred Haines, had a load of hanging meat on board from Shoulers abattoir at Carnaby destined for Bahu les Poiters in Rungis, the meat market in Paris. He shipped into Calais from Dover and as was normal he produced a non-quota permit, which only gave you a limited twenty-five kilometre radius from point of entry. Normally this worked, especially with a ten franc note tucked into the permit. This particular customs office rejected this approach and Fred, the most amenable, likeable guy going, produced a general quota permit. The customs officer immediately confiscated all his documents and impounded the truck with one helluva hefty fine. Fred didn't have that sort of money. Consequently he rang me late at night and the load of hanging meat missed the market.

In the early hours of the morning I had the dubious task of ringing Corine, a real tigress at Bahu, to tell her of the situation, and I got a real dressing down. This was followed by another one from Mr Shouler when I told him the same, to which he quite bluntly said, "If you haven't got the right papers et cetera then don't come back in here," although I reflect a few choice words were also used. The following morning I rang MAT Transport in Dunkerque, they paid the fine for me, and the lorry, with Fred and his wife Ann, was released so as to meet the following day's market; as one could have expected, the price of meat had gone down and Mr Shouler deducted this from my earnings from him.

My position at that time appeared dire as I had just bought, on finance, two meat hanging trailers to do the Shoulers job and there were no other prospects for them, and because I had just bought, again on a bank loan, Lodge Farm at Fraisthorpe as a new home and operating centre for my family and business. I felt at a new all-time low and a bit out of my depth. But like most things in life I wasn't down for long and every cloud has a silver lining.

After the Shouler incident, for some time I had a unit on for Fransen Transport based in Kidderminster, pulling one of their trailers. Fransen, a very reputable company with depots in Holland and Italy, offered me work from an abattoir at Shelly. This abattoir was licensed to slaughter horses and I did a first load to Rungis (Paris), Mick Francis did a second, the third we declined.

At that time the Cold War between the USA and Russia was at its height and President Carter banned all food exports to Russia, so they bought protein from Europe. As such, through Fransen, we took hanging meat to Nova Sad in Yugoslavia and loaded directly onto other trucks bound for Russia.

On one occasion, Clarrie Sutton and I were overnighting in Yugoslavia, freezing cold and snowbound. The following morning there was a knock on my cab door and there was a cup of tea for me followed by 'breakfast in ten minutes'. Clarrie had prepared in his cab kippers and scrambled eggs – scrumptious. What a lovely guy Clarrie is, one of the best around and an excellent driver, even though over his time with me we did have a few differences of opinion, mainly over the permit situation and some of my working methods. He, of course, was right, but you gotta do what you gotta do, and Clarrie somehow did it.

Because of my involvement with MAT Transport Ian McKinley, who was the French groupage manager, contacted me to contract two units every week to work into northern France in the Lille-Roubaix area on a mileage delivery loading rate. This proved excellent as, with a bit of ducking and diving, I could get away with using my non-25km quota permits by using the Dover-Dunkerque ferry and the infamous corridor route.

After eighteen months or so, as the trade built up, purely by Ian's efforts, we decided that Ian needed to upgrade his status. So after a meeting at a pub in Leven near Beverley, we formed B.B. Read Freight Forwarding Ltd. with Ian having a forty percent shareholding and me sixty, with the office at Fraisthorpe. This worked extremely well and Ian was excellent at what he did, providing expertise gained after many years at MAT Transport. He brought into the fold blue-chip companies such as ICI Fibres Wilton Ltd, for whom we undertook all the work to Greece, and Philips Components Ltd in Washington with loads destined for Italy, Spain, Germany, Austria and Holland. Ian employed owner/drivers as well as my own and in our heyday we had at any one time twenty-five to thirty lorries running under the B.B. Read banner. Certainly good rewarding days.

However, in the background was Thomas Hamlin Ltd, where the deep-sea fishing business was floundering and they had problems unknown to me. I had noticed deficiencies in my accounts and when I approached them I was fobbed off with some meaningless excuse, which I wouldn't accept. Consequently the relationship between my partners and I quickly evaporated and we were at loggerheads for approximately two years before I finally bought them out.

Money was not the contest, but previously I had bought a quarter share in an inshore trawler, the St Keverne. The skipper, Alan Kirkby, held a quarter share and Thomas Hamlin Ltd the remaining fifty percent. The trawler didn't really make any money, or so it seemed when I read the accounts. Eventually, because of engine failure, the boat was laid up for some considerable time. As was normal in the fishing game, the owners could apply for a grant to replace the old engine and I was asked to sign for my part, which I refused to do, as my dispute with Hamlins was at an all-time low. Obviously it looked very awkward and Alan came to see me to ask why I wouldn't sign as my reluctance was robbing him of his livelihood. To which I suggested that I would sell him my twenty-five percent holding, and I was no longer involved.

I don't think Hamlins approved of this, but nevertheless it opened the door for us to come to an agreement on B. B. Read. Like everything in life the infighting between me and Hamlins had an effect on Ian who was also having family problems, as his wife had left him. So Ian left me. But I must commend him, for even though he brought in the likes of ICI and Philips, he never poached them away from me, even though I'm pretty sure he could have done when he went to work with Britannia Freight in Hull. Thank you Ian; it was a sad loss to me and without him who knows how I would have prospered.

With Ian leaving this meant that I still had the day to day, trip to trip documentation to sort; we had a T1 T2 export custom TIR agreement which involved guarantees with the UK customs. This meant we had or could send goods to the continent, but leave ourselves open to any claim for undischarged documents which could involve thousands of pounds. Sourcing such documents with a valid excuse was extremely time-consuming, my workload increased dramatically and I found chasing the undischarged documents so challenging, which also took away the few trips that I so enjoyed when Ian was with me. My first love, as always, was driving my own trucks.

As time progressed, I employed Pat as my secretary and Dave, my son-in-law, to work in the office. Both proved competent so, much to my relief, I did the occasional trip. Every Friday night, week in week out, we shipped out via North Sea Ferries, a truck loaded from Philips Components to be in Barcelona for 7 a.m. on Monday morning. Whoever was the driver, after leaving Zeebrugge, would make for Montilimar service area south of Lyon and stay there until 10 p.m. Sunday night, to arrive in Barcelona the following morning. A ban on driving on a Sunday, unless carrying perishable goods, was in force and was strictly enforced by the French police.

On one occasion I had loaded ex Carcer in Spain a load of citrus fruit and I rang Dave to see who had shipped out on the Friday night and he told me Mick Frances. Knowing where he would be on the south side of Montilimar, on my way north I stopped and, sure enough, there was Mick parked up. Mick was one of the first drivers I employed and although renowned for being temperamental, he was also one of the most reliable drivers I have employed. When every other driver wouldn't go away, Mick would turn round and do the job and for that Mick, you were the best.

Anyway Mick, on this occasion, due mainly to my weird sense of humour where I took to going and inspecting and kicking his tyres, took offence and told me in no uncertain terms where to go. To which I went back to the northbound service area and enjoyed a petit-dejeuner on my own.

Although we loaded a lot of citrus fruits from the Murcia-Carcer area of Spain, one of the best loads back to the UK was from La Molet, a district of Barcelona, from Menorcina, an ice-cream manufacturing company, which produced ice-cream products resembling a coconut shell with coconut ice-cream in it, lemon in a lemon shell and so on. We brought the first pallet back to the UK for Messrs Brake Bros and secured a longstanding contract once these products proved popular; to their depots in Chelmsford, Swindon and South Kirby. A great company which remains a major food distribution company to this day. Fred even took Mr Brake's daughter's furniture and private belongings to Italy for her, such was the close liaison I was proud to have with their company.

The work from ICI Wilton more or less ended, apart from a rush job, as they found container traffic much cheaper than door to door overland transport. But as ever, another door always opened for me and I got a chance phone call from a John Page of H & P Freightings about a job to Gibraltar. The dispute between Spain and Gibraltar had ended to some degree and the barrier had been lifted allowing traffic to flow between them. The problem was that Safeways Superstore had its main duty free store in Gibraltar and sourced all its products from the UK, shipping via Ellesmere Port to Gibraltar but taking days to get there. Pegasus, a local shipping agent had the sole rights to both clearing customs and delivering the containers to the store.

The manager (who incidentally had worked at the Bridlington store) wanted a faster delivery service. John, his wife, Sandra and myself flew out to Gibraltar and as the guests of Safeway stayed at the Rock Hotel, the most prestigious hotel on the peninsula. It was my task to try and appoint an agent to clear customs from the landlocked Spanish border point at La Linea. Because Pegasus was, in my eyes, the local mafia and had control of the situation, all the agents shied away from my suggestions that they act for us. Having no success on this front I suggested to the manager of Safeways that I could have a lorry at the La Linea border crossing within three days from final collection and it was up to them to appoint an agent for their goods; this was met with approval.

So the first truck, driven by Mick Francis, did arrive at La Linea, cleared and delivered as per schedule. Pegasus immediately responded and brought in their own trucks and accordingly took over the job. I can only presume that the rate was more competitive than mine. But again this opened the door for a new customer, Transocean Enterprise. The owner was a Mr Abraham Cohen who had also been forced to use container traffic to receive his goods and now wanted to use the open door from Spain to Gibraltar. He was the appointed agent for the likes of McCain, Fox's Biscuits, Lyons Maid, Tate & Lyle, Winterbottom, Darby-Leisure Cooking Oils, et cetera. The job was lucrative to me and proved successful, backloading from southern Spain with produce, flowers, and more.

Although a very shrewd businessman he and his daughter Denise became friends and when his other daughter got married at the Park Lane Hotel on Piccadilly in London, Sandra and I were the only non-Jewish guests at the wedding, a really sumptuous affair – and I had to wear a skull cap!

One day Mr Cohen rang me: "Barry, I have bought a talking car in London and I want you to bring it here for me, but not to drive it here." So Derek Taylor, one of my drivers, loaded it into the back of a fridge, he then topped up his load at Leisure Oils in Dunkerque and drove down to Gibraltar.

We worked with Transocean Enterprises for a number of years and it was a very popular destination for all my drivers, and quite lucrative for me, backloading with fruit and flowers mainly. As time went by I was able to acquire four EEC books, which meant that I could do a three-legged journey, say loading ex-UK and delivering to Italy, reloading to Belgium, then reloading back to the UK. A whole new market.

Though our workload had grown, and we still held on to the work Ian had first produced, I reduced the number of owner/drivers who worked for us and subsequently gave loads outward-bound to other companies such as G Gilbert Transport from Boston, Mantons Transport from Harrogate, Ralph Davis from Cheltenham and others. Much easier for us, and less hassle as they were very reputable companies. I was approached by Gagewell Transport, who again I subcontracted work to, about joining them. They were quite a diverse company with three divisions: the green side did warehousing and distribution for ASDA (before ASDA set up their own system); the red side did high security distribution for the likes of Benson & Hedges and they were exceptionally good at this; and the blue side that they wanted to expand into continental temperature-controlled transport, which was where their interest in my company came in.

My thoughts at that time centred on the fact that road haulage was so competitive and you were only as good as your last job and as cheap as your next. Because our main customers were as blue chip as anyone, other companies bigger than mine were always approaching them with cheaper rates. So maybe it was better to be part of a bigger more diverse company; maybe that was the way forward.

A couple of meetings with Gagewell, with both solicitors and accountants present, led nowhere as agreement on values came amiss and I walked out. Then it looked like an agreement would not have transpired and all seemed lost. However, some time later Gagewell approached me again and further meetings were arranged at the solicitors' office in central Leeds. Eventually, after a lot of haggling by both sides, an agreement was reached and quite a large sum of money was offered to me on signing, with a similar amount delayed for twelve months hence. I would be employed as the International Transport Consultant in charge of day to day transport activities with targets to meet, and developing the business.

I could still operate for the time being at Fraisthorpe with Dave still employed in the office. They in turn sent a woman secretary every day from the Dewsbury area to Fraisthorpe to administer invoicing, banking, et cetera.

My immediate boss who I had to report to was a guy called Chris Fareham. I didn't like him and he certainly didn't like me. As part of my role I was to introduce him to my existing customers and on one such meeting with Brake Bros at their head office in Ashford, Kent, the guy I had dealt with for a number of years also took an instant dislike to him and told me so. On the way back home in his car on the M20 we fell out and I, in my rough and ready stupidity, told him to pull over on to the hard shoulder and sort it out, which for me was a punch-up.

After the weekend I was told to report to Gagewells' office in Dewsbury, as such behaviour was unworthy of the company's profile. Chris Fareham went in first to put his side of the dispute, I went in second and was asked to apologise and hopefully work together. Typical of me, I refused and said that not only that but his desk would be put in the middle of the yard at Fraisthorpe (which was still mine) and he could work from there. I really didn't know what to expect and I thought I was out of my depth here. But to my surprise they fired Chris Fareham and reprimanded me, saying that such behaviour from me would not be tolerated.

Things settled down for a time but, despite the constraints set by Gagewells, apparent with big companies, I nearly always did things my own way. Disconcern was shown by both parties. In my quest to find new business I secured a contract with Hutton Ship Stores in Hull; they were a large ship chandler with their own trucks serving cruise ships all over the continent. I had previously done some work with them over the years, so knew their business was very lucrative. Part of the contract meant renewing their fleet of trucks and trailers and moving my office from Fraisthorpe into a temporary cabin in their yard in Hedon Road, Hull. Quite an upheaval but for a time it worked. However, my relationships with the Gagewell managers were to say the least very strained.

I was asked to report to Dewsbury early one morning and as I walked into their office, unknown to me, they sent into the Hull office a couple of under-managers to search for whatever, and I was sacked for seemingly under-performing. My only excuse, which to me was valid, was that they were top-heavy with managers, all on a lucrative pay deal, and not putting a penny piece on the table. Anyway, I was out, rather pleased in one way, but concerned as to my future as my contract with them totally took away my involvement with any transport activities. On my way back home I went via Scarborough Hospital, where my daughter Frances had just given birth to Joe Cullen, my grandson. Sandra was there and I told her the news that I was out of work.

As my delayed payment wasn't due for another five to six months, I didn't, because of my contract, do anything in that time related to transport. Dave told me what had happened on that fateful day, that as I walked into the Dewsbury office, these other two guys entered the Hull office and consequently searched everything. As far as I am aware there was nothing to incriminate anyone. In the remaining few months, Dave, on his way back home from Hull told me of the decline that was taking place. Drivers who lived in the area also called and told me how much the job had deteriorated.

As my deferred payment day approached the M.D. of Gagewell, Stephen Cook, rang me and asked me if I wanted to buy back the business, and I agreed to buy back part of it from the deferred money due to me. At solicitor level this was agreed on, so under a new title, B. B. Read International I was back on the road with me in sole control. Strange how things work out, and I have always believed that I have someone watching over me pointing the way.

So we settled down again and a couple of new Renault Magnums were bought as were a couple of Lamberet fridge trailers, emblazoned with the new logo. Kevin, my son, came to drive for us as an owner/driver with a unit I sold to him.

On a trip to Gibraltar he was picking up various collections in the UK and loading ex Leisure Oils in Dunkerque; he also had to pick up twenty or so boxes of cheese from a company in Le Mans. As the customs office was closed and would not re-open until the Monday morning, we were faced with the decision on what to do:

wait until Monday or proceed to Gibraltar to reach the scheduled delivery for Monday. I tried to contact Mr Cohen by phone but got no answer. I knew he employed a gang of Moroccans to unload the truck when it arrived so was aware they would have been there on Monday morning without a truck to unload. So I decided that rather than wait until Monday to get T1 documents, the better way would be to let Kevin go without the appropriate documents, as it only involved such a small amount. There didn't seem to be a problem and Mr Cohen seemed pleased to have the truck there on the Monday and his gang unloaded accordingly. It was only some time later when he applied for a duty refund on the cheese without a T1 document that he showed his annoyance at my decision. Although I had the deepest respect for Mr Cohen I soon became aware of why the Jewish people are regarded as being money conscious. Unfortunately, we fell out and I only did one more job for him and he deducted the unclaimed duty money from my rate. Another lesson learned Barry.

Dave by now had passed his HGV test so went on the road as a regular driver. He and Frances were now divorced and some areas of the relationship were strained. Although Dave could be relied on for going away, turning round when needed, he was susceptible to a drink or two. On a trip loaded ex Philips he was coming off the Brittany Ferries ship at Caen when he turned the truck over, causing damage costing over £450,000, not to mention air cargo costs to Philips, as his load of deflection units were damaged and Philips in Dreux, France, where we delivered daily, were faced with production shutdown as each plant only stocked for a day to day production. Dave was slightly injured and taken to hospital, but no breathalyser test was taken as to his condition, although it was confirmed by others that he had been drinking on the overnight crossing.

Everyone is, I suppose, due one mistake, but some time later on a return trip from France loaded with apples for a Tesco delivery, he made the overnight sailing from Caen to Portsmouth on Brittany Ferries. Seemingly he was found fast asleep and worse for wear, the keys were taken off him and another driver drove his truck off

77

and parked it. As far as I am aware, or was informed, he was seen in his lorry attempting to drive away; a security guard tried to stop him, aware that he was incapable of doing so, but to no avail. As the lorry stopped at the security gatehouse, the police were informed and Dave was taken in to custody. Both Brittany Ferries and the police rang me and informed me that Dave had been arrested and the lorry locked in a secure compound, with the keys being kept at the police station. As the load of apples was treated as perishables and non-delivery as scheduled would result in a claim, I had no choice but to chase down to Portsmouth at nearly midnight with Nigel Orman, one of my drivers. Thankfully no claim was made, thanks to you Nigel. Dave was released the following day to make his own way home. I've hardly seen him since. Another lesson in trust Barry.

I guess I was losing confidence in the job; legislation, forever competing on price. It was to some extent taking its toll. As an example, the round trip work for McCain came under fire from a company called Marchnight who chopped the rate so much. They charged VAT but as far as I am aware never paid it over and I believe the VAT man closed them down.

I worked with a company from Newport near Hull, K Matthews, giving them loads on a round trip basis and as such he gave me work from Crystal Heart, who produced plants, from Howden to Lisbon, Portugal. This was a two-driver trip as the tomato plants had to be in Lisbon early in the morning of the third day of loading. An excellent company with lucrative rates. I got on well with Matthews and for a time deemed him a friend, although he was a bit flamboyant and drove a roller – not my scene at all. Although on a night out with him the car park man came up to us and told him over dinner that his Rolls Royce road tax was way out of date.

One of Matthews' contracts was from English Villages Salads to various supermarkets' distribution centres. Their policy changed and they would only accept fully loaded trucks rather than part loaded, and they had to go through Fowler Welch of Spalding. Consequently they lost the contract.

I was about ready for calling it a day and approaching sixty years old. I sold out to Matthews but remained as a consultant with certain duties. After fewer than six months it soon became apparent that the day to day transport manager resented my opinions, especially when two empty identical lorry and fridge trailers were passing each other in the opposite direction. So from going in on a daily basis it reduced to two then one day a week. Matthews went in to liquidation over a bank holiday period, but thankfully a couple of trailers I had on rent to them I got out before the liquidator went in after the holiday.

Matthews going bust caused quite a lot of bad feeling from companies owed money, as they thought I still had a financial holding in the company which I didn't. In particular, my sympathy lay with some of the owner/drivers who had worked for me, including my own son Kevin, who suffered financial hardship.

Philips, in particular, while constructing a rescue package asked me to sort something out for them which I did through one of my best friends in the industry, Pete Cook, who worked for Geoff Gilberts in Boston. To date, I believe Philips no longer exists in Washington and production of deflection units was transferred to Eindhoven in the Netherlands and G Gilberts are no longer there.

Away from the financial pressures of road transport, it was time to fully enjoy leisure time, my Goldwing 1500 motorbike and my Autotrail three-axle camper van. Although Lodge Farm at Fraisthorpe had been both our home and served us well for the business, the thought of nothing going on there depressed me, so I put it up for sale. After some to-ing and fro-ing negotiating a fair price we sold it to Mr & Mrs Kirkbright from Bradford. We had spotted a vacant plot on Martongate in Bridlington but by the time we were in a position to move on, the builder D Dunk had started to lay foundations. As he was retiring from building, we bought it and at the time of writing, live very happily in the most beautiful house and gardens. We also bought our fantastic villa at 845 Brighton Drive, Davenport in Highlands Reserve, a golf course location just off the US27 in Florida. We loved being there and would spend anywhere from four to six weeks there mainly in the autumn and winter months.

We made good friends with Dave and Karen, an English couple from Nottingham, who were trying to get their green card and residency papers. Things didn't go right for them and when the Twin Towers were hit all applications were halted. Unfortunately for Dave he was caught with only doing some minor work, but was picked up by the border control and deported. He suffered badly at the deportation prison in Panama City.

After this we decided to sell our villa. They had been our eyes and ears, as we did short-term lettings through the management company I.P.G., and at times, seemingly, some of the guests were somewhat dubious. One such letting was to a family from the UK who completely trashed the place, however I.P.G. did renew everything apparently at no cost to us, but I often wondered.

I really enjoyed our home in Florida and on most occasions while visiting we would fly via Delta Airlines into Atlanta, Georgia and then drive to Florida on different routes. On one such drive we had our friends Dave and Jo Price with us and after an overnight stay in Atlanta we drove to Chattanooga, Nashville, Memphis and New Orleans before ending up at our villa five days later. It was a wonderful experience taking in the music scene and the historical rock and roll memorabilia.

I loved Florida and explored it as much as possible, going to its southern tip Key West, to Naples, a very expensive and upmarket city, taking the Tami-Ami Trail north to St Petersburg, Tampa and back to our villa. Hotels for overnight stops are plentiful and reasonable, and the accommodation more than adequate. Yes, a good time, and I was sad when I sold it, but whoever would have thought I would own a home in America. I wish my mum and dad could have seen it.

Who knows, maybe they could, after all my mum's dad was an American G.I. from the First World War. He was stationed at Driffield R.A.F. airfield, met my gran, and hey-ho, my mum was the product of a whirlwind romance. My gran's parents were not impressed and literally turned her out. She walked all the way from

Driffield to Bridlington, some twelve miles, and entered the workhouse, the only refuge available to her, and consequently my mum was born (Virginia May Wise); a stigma she carried all her life, being born in a workhouse. A thought I always had, but never confirmed, was that my G.I. grandfather was a Virginian from that state in America and so my gran christened her Virginia.

Late in her life, I bought the rented house where I grew up at 18 Havelock Crescent, Bridlington. It consisted of or rather was devoid of a bathroom, an outside toilet across the yard, one solitary cold water tap and a scullery where my mum did her chores et cetera. Bath time was usually on Friday nights in a tin bath that hung behind the scullery back door and was shared by all, obviously individually, topped up with hot water from the kettle that had boiled on the open fire. I was prompted to buy the house after my mum fell in the back yard while going to the outside loo. My intention was to upgrade the house with a bathroom and inside loo by knocking down the coal house and outside loo.

I completed the purchase in the August of 1988, but mum died on December 12th that year, and so never got the pleasure she so rightly deserved. I loved my mum: beautiful in her younger days, kindness itself, dreadful with money although she never had much to start with, but if she had she would have given it away. Most of what we had was what we called 'on tick', and many times there would come a knock on the front door from the man referred to as 'The Tadman'. Mum would say to me, tell him I am not in and will pay him next week. I don't really know if I was a convincing liar, but he would go away, uttering some remarks along the lines of 'and I will be back next week'. We even got fish and chips on tick from Mr Charters on Quay Road through the week and then would pay for them on a Friday or Saturday night, when dad got paid, and then the process would start again the following week.

Life was simple, but everyone was the same down Havelock Crescent and a good friendly atmosphere existed. Yes, not an easy time but one that has taught me the value of what I have today and how fortunate I have been to achieve them.

After selling my Florida villa, for a short period of time I wasn't too happy just kicking my heels. Sandra and I had done a round-the-world trip, in particular really enjoying our rail journey on the Indian-Pacific Gold Class railway from Perth to Adelaide then the Ghan from Adelaide to Alice Springs, then Cairns to Brisbane and Sidney to Melbourne, in Australia, returning home via Honolulu and California – a really enjoyable trip lasting six weeks. Other rail trips included one on the Rocky Mountaineer from Calgary to Vancouver in Canada, where we stayed a couple of days with my very good friend, Chris Teale. We then hired a car and Sandra and I toured most of British Colombia.

However, my love of the open road prevailed and I bought a brand new Autotrail Chieftain, three-axle motorhome, and we travelled extensively throughout the UK, Germany, Italy and many trips to Spain. Eventually I exchanged my Autotrail for a Mercedes Rapido; this was beautiful and because of the V6 engine was extremely powerful. For reasons I am not sure about I sold this to Martins of Exeter and although having turned round twice to come back, decided to go through with the sale and returned home by train.

I loved my Goldwing 1500, painted black with planets and stars highlighted on it, but decided to exchange it for an 1800 Goldwing, with a dealer in Doncaster and made the changeover en route to a Treffen (camping meet) week in Carmarthen, South Wales. At first I wasn't sure I had done the right thing, but now I have added my bits and pieces to enhance it, I love it and it sure looks good. We have been on several Treffens, my favourite always being Kelso in Scotland, a lovely place with friendly people.

One day my son Kevin said, "How would you like to go as a second driver with a company called Redburn Transfer on a Phil Collins tour?" I wasn't too sure as I expected a few weirdos, but thought what the hell! So we left home at midnight in Kev's Evo, first stop Howden to drop off a DVD for one of his mates and a quick pee, only to be confronted by two police officers, to whom I stupidly said that we had just dropped off some gear. They took a look in the back of the car, we told them we were going on tour, and they wished us good luck.

The tour went really well and I enjoyed the experience and made good friends with my driver, Peter Cramp. He was very experienced and enthusiastic and a first class driver. I had many tours after that including with Queen, where I flew out to Moscow in Russia then Riga in Latvia, Warsaw in Poland, then Hamburg and Paris. Also, Kings of Leon, Simply Red and at least six with Bruce Springsteen, certainly one of my favourite bands, The Eagles, definitely my favourite, and Chicago, who were so friendly to me and invited me to join them at dinner. A lot of the trips were in Scandinavia and I had many experiences, which I have recorded on a daily basis in my journals, for whoever cares to read them.

Talking of experiences: there was one trip I did with Kevin in his left-hand-drive Volvo, when he was subcontracting for Eddie Stobart on NAAFI work in Kosovo when the former Yugoslavia war was at its height. I went as a passenger for a jolly really. As Yugoslavia couldn't be transited as the war spread through Kosovo, Serbia, and Bosnia, transit had to be back from Greece. The route went from Ancona to the Ingonisa ferry, then to the military camp at Pristina, then an M.P. escort to the delivery point. Unfortunately, and stupidly, Kevin had an incident with a car driver en route. The driver looked like he was going to attack Kevin, so in Kevin's defence, I hit this guy with a baseball bat that Kevin kept in his cab. The guy was a bit of a mess but he got up, drove off and the next time we saw him he was at a military roadblock presumably reporting us. Nothing happened as we had seen roadside makeshift graves for locals who had perished in the conflict. Later we found out that a Turkish driver had been shot and killed for such a traffic incident. The rest of the day and the return trip back to the Greek border were uneventful, but I have to admit I was concerned in case of a reprisal. I did get the name 'Barry the Bat' from the other drivers with us. A return load from Italy and we came back home. Kevin refused to take me again – I can't see why?

Snowbound in Norway.

Caught and fined by Spanish police.

Delivering chips from McCains in Scarborough to a cold store in Kesteren, Holland when I was on contract with Hull Ships Stores.

Photo shoot for Transport magazine showing the old ship *Norsea* for NS ferries.

Left hand drive Turkish spec DAF 3300 6x2 rear lift axle. Bound for Italy loaded with fish from Scotland.

My first Renault Magnum L77 BBR. A photo shoot by Thompsons of Beverley on Bridlington seafront.

Breakdown at Como, Italy. Piggyback home for repair.

Just taking a 45-minute break.

DAF Space Cab 6x2 3300. Ironically this was blessed by our local vicar in Fraisthorpe before going out one Sunday morning on its first trip. Two years later it burnt out to a cinder near Caen in France.

Home base at Fraisthorpe.

A blown trailer super single tyre - note the damage.

A Renault Magnum that turned over in France. The cab was renewed but the trailer was a write-off as was the load of deflection units. Claim was in excess of £450,000.

Waiting to load oranges at Carcer, Spain. Given the job as tractor driver while waiting.

A lunchtime stop somewhere in Yugoslavia bound for a ship in Greece.

91

At Peterborough Truck Show - won best livery award.

Me with a typewriter as an office bound boy. Note the stored tacho charts.

Kevin's Volvo with B.B. Read International. Trailer en route to Portsmouth-Caen ferry.

Redburn Transfer. Parked at The Globe in Gothenburg for The Eagles.

On tour with Queen for Redburn Transport en route from Moscow, Russia to Riga in Latvia. Road was atrocious.

My Rapido motorhome - don't know why I sold it!

My lovely 1500 Goldwing painted with planets and stars.

Tilt trailer, mainly for groupage to Italy and Greece.

Me with Gordon banks, goalkeeper for England when winning the World Cup.

All my biking mates at Sherburn in Elmet.

READ KEEPS HIS COOL

Barry Read was one of the best known names in international reefer haulage. He's retired now, but as Nick Garlick found, he's kept an immaculate Scania and runs a high-profile motor cycle

During a recent visit to Yorkshire, I asked a friend what had happened to Barry Read International from Bridlington and his well turned out fleet. 'Oh that's easy,' my friend replied. 'He retired three years ago and sold the company to another local haulier. But don't worry, he kept a Scania 112 coupled to a fridge trailer.'

One phone call later I was on my way to Fraisthrope on the North Yorkshire coast to meet Read and his immaculate truck Even on a dull, damp day it looked resplendent in blue and white, adorned with extra lights, stainless-steel accessories, polished aluminium wheels and hooked to a matching trailer.

As Read showed me round he remarked: 'The most noticeable difference from other Scanias is the high-roof conversion that I believe was the first Estepe in the country... it was fitted from new. Although not as obvious, another item that makes this vehicle unique is the conversion from a twin-steer to a mid-lift. All the drag links have been removed, tidying up the chassis.

'This is still the original paint job and a lot of credit has to go to Fred Haynes, the driver who had the wagon from new,' he added. The immaculate interior is in original Scania light blue trim, which extends up into the high-roof.

Barry with the truck he took into retirement. Note the distinctive livery

The Scannie's looks are matched by its smooth-running 333hp engine. With more than a million miles on the clock it's had a reconditioned block, but the gearbox and drive axle are original.

EXCELLENT RELIABILITY

Reliability has been excellent, when the engine was turned off we could even hear the oil spinner winding down – not bad for a vehicle first registered in August 1987.

Side air deflectors let the stripes flow from the tractor to the Lamberet trailer, where side skirts contribute to the artic's smooth lines.

Read was moving house when I visited him so the trailer was loaded with furniture and suits were hanging from the cab ceiling. But it was the chandelier that really caught my eye: it must make this the smartest temperature-controlled removal truck in the UK – unless you know better?

Retired now but a fitting end to my years as an owner/operator.

99

Chapter Ten
Holidays

I, or should I say we, have had some fabulous holidays staying in some of the very best hotels in the world, including: The Belagio in Las Vegas with its frontline views overlooking the fountains rising and falling to whatever music is played; the Renaissance in Naples, Florida; Sails in the Desert in Ayres Rock, Australia; and many more, which again I have highlighted in my day to day journals. But at the same time I have made some dreadful decisions, probably the worst of which was in Key West, Florida, namely the Spanish Gardens, a drive-in motel that was dreadful and to some extent a bit scary as the clientele were somewhat dubious. But I was in such a haste to watch the sunset from the most southern point in Florida, my judgement in selecting a hotel failed me.

I have driven thousands of miles in the USA, thankfully accident-free and really without incident. Driving there in comparison to the UK is much more relaxing. The longest journey we took was from Las Vegas to Orlando, Florida, some 2,000 miles via Phoenix, Arizona, New Orleans, across the panhandle to Orlando and eventually Key West. The idea was to meet Joanne and family in Orlando and spend Christmas together but unfortunately they couldn't get out of Manchester as it was snowbound. So we were left with the prospect of spending Christmas, just the two of us, in a five bedroom villa I had previously booked. By chance one of my biking friends, Neil Gowland, was on holiday with his family so I invited them up for Christmas Day; Sandra conjuring up some nibbles and then all of us going down to the celebration in Market Street which was like a magical wonderland and where it snows on the hour, every hour with man-made soap flakes. The Christmas dinner we shared was pizza, as all of the restaurants were fully booked.

Probably the most relaxing and interesting holidays have been our rail journeys, on one of which we stayed at Raffles Hotel in Singapore; another fabulous place where Sandra had her photograph taken with the Rhaj , who took a shine to her. Then we flew on to Perth, Australia and stayed a couple of nights there. Incidentally I loved Fremantle, where we arrived after a cruise on the Swan river. Then we caught the Indian-Pacific Gold Class train to Adelaide; two nights on the sleeper with the most excellent cuisine and well-equipped cabin. We met some very interesting people, one of whom was on her own, namely Carol Beal from Canada, and we still keep in touch by exchanging Christmas cards.

We met up with Paul Brown in Adelaide, the son of my friend Bobby Brown and he took us to his home and introduced us to his family and then back to our lovely hotel next to the Australian cricket ground. We then caught the Ghan train that took us to Ayres Rock, or Uluru as the locals call it. Hence the Sails in the Desert hotel, which was beautiful. I can't say I liked the area at all; just swarms of flies converging in your hair, mouth, eyes and ears – horrible – but what was intriguing was the sunset on Ayres Rock. We then took a coach trip to Alice Springs, another place I didn't like at all as the Aborigines were far from friendly, and unkempt.

From there we flew to Cairns, which was quite harrowing as we had an emergency landing when the landing leg doors wouldn't close and the turbulence was horrendous. We had to circle the airport five times to burn up the fuel before going in to land. Thankfully all ended well. From Cairns we went to Brisbane and Sydney where we stayed on Bondi Beach. Quite by chance it was Australia Day on the Sunday and we went and took part in the celebrations – a wonderful day. From there to Melbourne, a lovely city where we stayed in the St Kilda district, our hotel overlooking the ocean with the most wonderful sunsets. Back to Sydney then a flight to Honolulu where we crossed the international time zone and ended up a day back on ourselves.

They say never go back on what you hold as magical, and Honolulu was not the same as the first time we visited when we went some years before for a trucking convention – it's now so commercialised. From there we flew to Los Angeles where we stayed for three nights on the old Queen Mary which is now out of commission and serves as a hotel at Long Beach, Santa Barbara. It was nice although a bit old hat, but I suppose years ago it was the height of luxury. We did a private executive car tour of L.A. where we were shown all the film stars' houses. The driver was very entertaining, but at the same time full of crap, but we enjoyed his banter and I tipped him well.

From there I hired a car and we drove north stopping on the first night at a hotel in Santa Barbara owned by Fess Parker, the guy who played Davy Crockett in the film. It was a lovely hotel, expensive, but worth it. Which is more than I can say for the city centre, as when I went for a walk on my own I was surprised at the number of hobos and drifters. The next day's drive on HNY1 along the Big Sur, which runs at the side of the Pacific Ocean, I can only describe as fabulous. By nightfall and in torrential rain we arrived at Carmel, the home of my fantasy movie sweetheart Doris Day and the mayor of Carmel, Clint Eastwood. For reasons I never found out Carmel has no street lighting and no house numbers. Trying to find a hotel proved fruitless and we faced the prospect of spending the night in the car. However, I decided to drive north again and found a rather dubious motel in Monterrey, by which time it was midnight.

The following morning, after a quick look round Monterrey which is basically like Grimsby and a whale and fish canning factory town, we drove back to Carmel and eventually found a very expensive hotel. The reason why there was such a hike in hotel prices was that it was the ITT golf championship finals at Pebble Beach and hotels were booked up years in advance, so we were lucky. Sandra told me off for being an idiot when I saw this blonde woman jogging and I ran after her shouting, "Doris, I'm here." Needless to say she looked away and quickened her pace. We did find her hotel though and had a drink and a sandwich there, and looked at all the memorabilia from her films that were hanging on the walls. At least I felt close to her and it was somewhat magical. We also had a drink and evening meal in the pub owned by Clint Eastwood called The Hog's Breath.

The following day the weather was still raining so I suggested we go to Las Vegas, and off we went. Instead of taking the interstates we again went south along the Big Sur and then over a mountain pass on a road that had snow at the top and then into a valley in which the road shimmered with heat glare and was so quiet for other traffic that the driver of a car coming towards us hung out of the side window to wave at us.

That night we arrived at Bakersfield and easily found a nice hotel. The next day after an early start we again chose the most indirect route only just bypassing Death Valley, the hottest place in the USA. When we finally arrived in Las Vegas it was late in the evening and again all the hotels were extremely busy as it was Valentine's Day. We had stayed before at the Mandalay Bay Hotel so that was the preference as the Luxor, where we had also stayed previously, was full. I sent Sandra in to see if she could get a room as she had sustained a broken wrist before we left home. The receptionist took pity on her and offered us a suite – very, very expensive, but we took it gladly. It was beautiful with wonderful views over the strip.

We had a couple of days in Las Vegas then decided to go to San Diego. At one point Sandra shouted out, "Look, Roy Rogers Boulevard." Sure enough here we were in Apple Valley, so we took off on to it and saw in front of us Roy Rogers' Hall of Fame, which resembles an old-style US cavalry fort with a large statue of Trigger, his horse, rearing up. We spent at least three hours looking around all the memorabilia of Roy and his wife Dale Evans who, apart from the fame they got from the good cowboy films they made, had quite a tragic life. I was mesmerised, especially with the car that Roy drove, which was at least twenty feet long from front to back and had six guns for door handles, and had a trailer hitched to the back for Trigger. On leaving I signed and commented in the visitor book. When Sandra asked me what I had put I said, with a lump in my throat and a sob, "Wonderful memories of a schoolboy hero." The lady behind the desk said, "Gee that's nice." A wonderful moment.

We had more problems finding a hotel in San Diego, again late into the evening, and guess what, it was Presidents' Day, so again all the hotels hiked up their prices. We eventually found one which at one time had been a bank and our room resembled a bank vault; unusual but quite unique. San Diego is a beautiful city with very much a Mexican flavour throughout, as we were near to the Mexican border at Tijuana. Also, very much to my interest, this was where Wyatt Earp, the renowned lawman and Marshall of Tombstone of 'Gunfight at the OK Corral' fame, finally retired to, and the Gaslight area portrays his legend. We crossed by foot into Tijuana for a time to savour the influence. I liked it but it wasn't for Sandra.

We then drove back to L.A., turned in the hire car and flew back home. It was a wonderful world trip – who would have thought that we would see and experience so much.

Tombstone – now that brings back another memory. On a previous trip to the USA we flew via Atlanta to Phoenix, Scotsdale then drove via Flagstaff through the Zion National Park and Carson City into Las Vegas, where we stayed over at the Mandalay Bay Hotel for a few days then drove, there and back, to the southern ridge of the Grand Canyon – 720 miles in one day. At night time we watched all the action in the casino until the early hours.

Leaving Las Vegas en route via the Hoover Dam we stayed over at Lake Havesue where the original London Bridge was reconstructed over the Colorado river and a replica of Big Ben was built. As I was told, the guy who bought the bridge thought he was buying our Tower Bridge. Nevertheless, a lovely place to visit. Our destination was Palm Springs, a really lovely upmarket town where the film stars of yesteryear i.e. Bob Hope and Frank Sinatra had streets named after them. The town is ringed by mountains and we took a lift up to the top and took in the views.

Yeah, Tombstone, a mythical wild-west town of gunfights, saloons, the Clantons, Doc Holliday, Big-Nose Kate, Ringo – the list is endless. We found a hotel on the edge of town called Lookout Lodge, where we sat outside warmed by an open-pit fire looking at the range of mountains in the distance only spanned by an endless stretch of barren wasteland. Our imagination was tested when we saw a cloud of dust growing ever closer to us, but as it got nearer all that appeared was a pick-up truck. But all I could think about was the Apache Indian renegade chief, Chocise who was holed up in the mountains and made attacks on the settlers in the region, pillaging and murdering as they went. That dust cloud in those days must have been horrendous. Oh my imagination!

I went to Boot Hill cemetery in Tombstone and the inscriptions on the gravestones were intriguing. The one that really amused me was the one saying: 'Two Fingers Jack died in a gunfight.' I don't think he stood a chance.

The Mexican border at Nogellas was quite nearby so we went for the day. What amused me on the US side was a Woolworths store with a Mexican truck delivering to it. I spoke with the driver for a time. Crossing into Mexico was quite easy; Sandra didn't like it at all as there was a strange atmosphere about it and we were accosted by a young guy who wouldn't take 'go away' for an answer and offered us everything from booze, drugs and a woman (his sister) for me. We didn't stay long, but getting back into the USA was a different story and we were grilled by the customs officer. Staying at the hotel was an Irish couple and they had gone to a different border and had extreme difficulties getting back into the USA as seemingly the IRA had been recruited to train Bolivian terrorists and, them being Irish, the authorities took a dim view of them going into Mexico. When we met up with them at night they certainly looked bedraggled.

I suppose I could go on about holidays and events but again each day is listed in my journals.

While I was an owner/driver with just one lorry (VAG 37S) and working directly for McCains loading ex Scarborough for Kesteren in the Netherlands, I made friends with Alan Woods Snr. who had a six-wheel rigid DAF, also working for McCains. He would, every Sunday, load a stock transfer from Scarborough for Whittersy and then work out of Whittersy for the rest of the week. He traded as Filey Freights and if anyone ever deserved a regular contract then Alan certainly did, as the facilities at Whittersy were pretty poor. As time went on he was joined by his son, Alan Woods Jnr., and Alan expanded the company with at least three artics and eventually began working for a company called D'Arta based in

Ardooie in Belgium, where he would ship out with an empty trailer, pick up a loaded one and then deliver to wherever in the UK. Whenever Alan needed time off, I would take one of his trucks and do the same. I enjoyed this and when D'Arta wanted a couple of trips to Italy then I was happy to oblige. Steven, my grandson, also worked for him and was proud that he also did the same trips. Tragically, for reasons not entirely clear to any of us, Alan Jnr committed suicide by hanging himself in his truck one night while parked at the Belgian-French border at Steenavorde. Whatever possessed him to do this? One can only imagine how troubled his mind must have been. Such a lovely guy and Alan Snr. would have been horrified, but by now he had passed on, so thankfully he would never know. But who knows what lies in the grand scale of the unknown?

Barry and Sandra on holiday in Marbella, Spain c.1987.

Barry and Sandra on holiday in Honolulu c. 1986.

Chapter Eleven
Models

By now I had retired and none of my former trucks were on the road. I had supposed that I had faded into obscurity, when I got a call from Corgi who make model trucks and are world famous. They wanted to produce a replica model of one of my trucks and trailers – as a gift to their fellow members. The one they chose was a Volvo FH which was actually Kevin's but with my trailer and all with the livery of B. B. Read International. They made 2,404 in 1:75 scale and sent them worldwide. The replica model is superb with every detail, and to say the least I was highly delighted and humbled. If only mum and dad could have seen. My friend Chris Teale who lives in Kelowne, Canada rang me and said, "Hey Readie, my next door neighbour has just received from Corgi a model of one of your trucks." It doesn't get much better than that.

A couple of years or so after this, Teckno, an Anglo-Dutch model-maker, contacted me as they wanted to create a 1.50 scale model of my old Scania 141 and fridge trailer in the livery of B. B. Read & Co. Their creation is superb, even sporting a roof rack and ladders with what looks like beer crates lodged in the rack. Brilliant, and once again I was humbled. These went on to the internet for sale at a recommended price of £180.00 each and sold, as a limited edition, a total of 150 models. As far as I am aware they were sought after and soon sold out.

Teckno, at a later date, came back and asked for details of one of my Scania 112 units with matching fridge trailer, this time in the livery of B. B. Read International. This again was made as a 150 limited edition and sold, as far as I am aware, for £200.00 upwards. Again they were sought after and soon sold. They did a fantastic job and I am highly delighted and complimented.

I have kept for my own pleasure some of the three models and they are on display in my games room, alongside the numerous other models I have. Two of my most prized possessions are a Garonne Lady and a Marseilles Lady. These were the tin-plated, gorgeous-looking ladies from: Garonne TIR Station, where I was on the night Garonne first opened in the outskirts of Paris adjacent to Le Bourget airport; and my Marseilles lady from a renowned truckstop in that city. Most of the drivers who were fortunate to get them both, adored them on the front grille of their trucks, but in no time they rusted up and were lost. I didn't, instead putting them inside my truck, and both are perfect to this day. I love my models and most days cast my enviable eye over them and think of yesteryear, and how much I loved and lived those days.

At the time of writing, Teckno has requested a photo of one of my space cab DAFs with the three-axle matching B.B. Read & Co. refrigerated trailer. Here's hoping; it will be a real bonus if they produce this. All in all I must have seventy or so models, mostly from the real veterans of yesteryear when, to me, truck driving meant truck driving.

Chapter Twelve

Now in my late seventies, but thankfully very fit and active, although I had to have a left knee replacement, my ambitions have never faltered. My son-in-law (Vince) asked me to go with him to Maritime's base in Tilbury, where he bought a DAF tractor unit and went to work for them on a contract basis. To me it sounded a real good deal and an excellent company to work for, although I believe the money aspect wasn't great.

He then bought a Mercedes van from near Harlow, which I went with him to buy, and then had a contract with DPD – long hours, no money, or not enough for the work involved. I bought the van from him and had it converted into a camper van to my own design: light bars, running side bars complemented the look and I had decals made up saying 'My Way'. I love my van and it certainly turns a few heads. To me it respects the days when driving meant you slept when tired, ate when hungry and drove for eternity. For reasons relating to Sandra's health it is not used to its full capacity, although I really enjoy going to all the relevant truck and motorhome shows in it.

My grandson Steven, a great guy of whom I am immensely proud, from the age of thirteen worked in a local garage and gained his apprenticeship qualifications, not to mention being the youngest M.O.T. graduate of his year. Now, with some financial help from me, he has struck out in the transport and repair industry as Dale & Read. His partner Mark is a real genuine guy who can turn his talents to both paint-spraying and renovation. They make a great team and with Mark's dad Dickie should hopefully make a success of their business. Hard work is something they are certainly prepared to undertake. They have suffered a few setbacks as two of the Scanias they first bought suffered serious engine breakdowns, but resilience helped them to come out the other side. And, to date, running two top-line Scanias and one Volvo with their own trailers they have regular work on a daily basis. The paint-spraying work is certainly busy and they have completed numerous resprays on both tractor units and trailers. In fact their finished work is so good I've had my Mercedes Sprinter camper sprayed at the bottom end and I am highly delighted with the finished job. So we may look forward to Dale & Read Transport being as successful as I certainly was. Good luck to them.

Kevin seems reasonably happy with what he is doing. He formed K+S Transport Ltd and hires himself out to various companies as a part-time HGV driver and has vast experience in all forms of transport, having gained qualifications in H.D.R., car carrying, continental work et cetera. He is currently enjoying prestigious work with Air India on Formula One transportation to all the Formula One circuit meetings, both in the UK and on the continent. And, of course, when at home he is a member of the Bridlington Lifeboat team. His great-granddad Pashby would have been immensely proud of him for that, as both Sandra and I are.

So life's been good to us. A few setbacks, some sadness, but one helluva lot of happiness and good times. Unfortunately, Sandra's health is an issue, both physically and now finding herself being diagnosed with slight dementia, and we are not sure where we will go with that. But we are all of us there for her, as she has been for all of us; a truly wonderful person, wife, mother and grandmother, and of course now a great-grandma.

We have been blessed with a lovely family whom we love and are loved by in return and we are most thankful for that. So although I first said to Sandra, "Don't get too serious about me," hell, I'm certainly glad she did.